POWERPOINT FOR DUMMIES

MICROSOFT POWERPOINT FOR BEGINNER'S

A Fundamental Guide to Mastering Microsoft PowerPoint for Beginners With Step by Step Illustrations

BONIFACE BENEDICT

DEDICATION

This book is dedicated to all computer lovers all over the world.

COPYRIGHT

Do not use any part of this book in any form – electronic, mechanical or physical without an express written permission from the author.

In case of any reference to any content in this book you should make adequate reference.

POWERPOINT FOR DUMMIES

TABLE OF CONTENTS

DEDICATION ii
COPYRIGHT iii
Chapter 1 1
PowerPoint Basics 1
   Uses of PowerPoint 1
   Starting your PowerPoint 3
   Working with Ribbons 4
   Working in the backstage view 9
   Opening an existing presentation 10
   Views in PowerPoints and their uses 11
   Creation and Editing Views 11
   Presentation Views 13
   Printing your Presentation 13
Chapter 2 14
Understanding Slide Layouts, Themes, and Placeholders 14
Types of Slide layout 15
   Applying a slide layout 18
   Editing and Reapplying Slides 18

Changing an existing layout.. 19
Renaming Layout... 20
Choosing a theme for your presentation 24
Using multiple themes in a presentation 25
Apply a theme to existing slides. 29
Creating themes in PowerPoint.. 30
Changing theme colors 31
Changing theme fonts 32
What is a PowerPoint template? 34
Types of Layout 36
Working with Objects... 39
Working on Text Objects.. 41

Chapter 3 43
Slides... 43
Inserting New Slide... 44
Importing Slides.. 47

Chapter 4 55
Writing and Formatting Text 55
Making use of Formatting toolbar 60
Changing Text Case.. 61
Indention 63
PowerPoint List Limitations 80
Common Problems Faced by Newbies and solutions.............. 81
Stopping the creation of numbers and bullets.................. 82

Chapter 5 85

Adding Sauce to your Work 85

    Working with Tables.. 85

    Inserting a table... 87

    Adding rows and columns 89

    Modifying tables with the Layout tab 90

    Working with Charts and Graphs in PowerPoint............................. 91

        Inserting a Chart 91

        Using Chart tools to customize your Chart..................... 93

        Changing Chart Style 95

Chapter 6 96

Adding Sauce to your Work II 96

    Working with Shapes.. 96

    Formatting shapes and text boxes. 98

    Changing the style of a shape 99

    Changing the outline of a shape.. 100

    Working with SmartArt Graphic 102

    Inserting a SmartArt graphic... 102

    Adding, Deleting and Rearranging shapes: 104

    SmartArt Customization 105

Chapter 7 107

Images, Videos and Animations 107

    How to Insert Images in PowerPoint 107

        How to Rotate an Image in PowerPoint 110

Videos 112
    Inserting a video from a file: 112
    How to make use of Screen recording 113
    Inserting online videos: 113
  Editing and formatting videos 114
  Animations 117
Chapter 8 124
Finalizing your work 124
  Using the Spell check Feature 124
  Automatic spell check 125
  Modifying proofing options 126
  Commenting on presentations 127
    Viewing comments 128
    Deleting comments 128
Chapter 9 132
Now that you are done 132
  Creating a PDF 133
  Saving your presentation on USB flash drive or CD 134
  Save your package to a USB flash drive 136
  Save as Video 137
  Save as a PowerPoint Show 139
Chapter 10 Work like a Guru 140
  7 Quick tips to make your Presentation more effective 140
PowerPoint shortcut 141

For windows.. 141
For MacOS... 142

Chapter 1

PowerPoint Basics

PowerPoint is a software application used for data and information presentation using animation, images, effects, etc. It is designed for information visualization. This helps people understand an idea easily. Just as Word documents are made up of pages, PowerPoint presentations are made up of slides. Slides contain graphics, animations, text, and other information.

With PowerPoint, you can create presentations and also use it to present them and the good thing is – you can use different media to show your presentations. Examples of media you can use include a Computer projector, Webcast (yeah show your presentation over the internet), computer screen, printed pages, etc.

Now that you know what PowerPoint is let us move to the uses of PowerPoint

Uses of PowerPoint

The use of PowerPoint cuts across different industries and has various uses. Here are a few of the numerous uses of PowerPoint.

Education: Teachers use PowerPoint to present and teach lessons. With the use of PowerPoint, it is easier for teachers to reinforce an important point by just highlighting those points in their slides. It also helps students create slides for personal learning study.

Business: business is all about strategies and these strategies are created based on data available. PowerPoint is a great tool for presentation. It helps you save time and protect your data and strategies easily. Speaking to a lot of people and making sure they understand fully all you are saying can be difficult. With PowerPoint all you have to do is visualize your data, this makes it easy to carry everyone along.

Job seekers: the knowledge of PowerPoint can make a job-seeker stand out. With the use of PowerPoint jobs, seekers can create a digital resume or a multimedia resume. This is a very creative and unique way of presenting your skills and knowledge before your interviewers.

Internet Presentation: so you have a presentation to make and you are worried your audience is in a different part of the word. Do not worry. PowerPoint can help you to set up a presentation that you can broadcast over the internet so people can join in without leaving the comfort of their homes.

Starting your PowerPoint

Press the windows keys of your keyboard. The window key is the key that has the window flag slammed on it. It is always beside the Alt key. This will make the start page pop up, where you will fill your commonly used applications. You might find the PowerPoint at the top and if not scroll down the start screen.

Click on the PowerPoint 2016 title

Boom you are in. The PowerPoint will start just in seconds.

If that doesn't work with your PC due to the window version of your PC, there is an alternative move your mouse to the search icon on your PC (this is usually at the bottom left corner on your screen, beside the window icon) and type PowerPoint.

Navigating PowerPoint

At this point I want you to sit back and grab a cup of coffee as you are about to be introduced to the nitty-gritty of what PowerPoint is all about.

Now let's begin.

Your PowerPoint is now up, and you are ready to create a presentation. All you have to click is the blank presentation (green arrow in) and then edit the blank presentation to your liking.

- **Choose Blank Presentation**: double-tap blank presentation to start afresh.
- **Pick a Template**: There are several templates displayed on the screen you can pick any of your choices.
- **Search template**: if you are not satisfied with the template displayed, you can type a search phrase into the search box. Double-tap any template you want.

Working with Ribbons

The ribbon is PowerPoint's major interface tool. It is a strip containing virtually all the commands you need to work with your slides and the good thing is that- it helps you find the tool that will help you complete your task easily.

What can you find on the Ribbon tab?

The ribbon label matches group tools and features together based on their uses. For example, if you want to spice up your slide and you click insert, you would see different options such as shapes, videos. There are 9 sections in the ribbon.

1) **Home**

The home tab contains the cut, copy and paste feature, font and paragraph feature, and every other thing you need to add and organize your slide.

POWERPOINT FOR DUMMIES

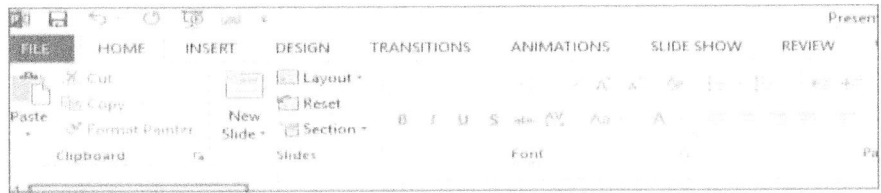

2) **Insert**

If you wish to add anything to your slide. Click insert. Different features will pop up which include- tables, pictures, shapes, charts and more

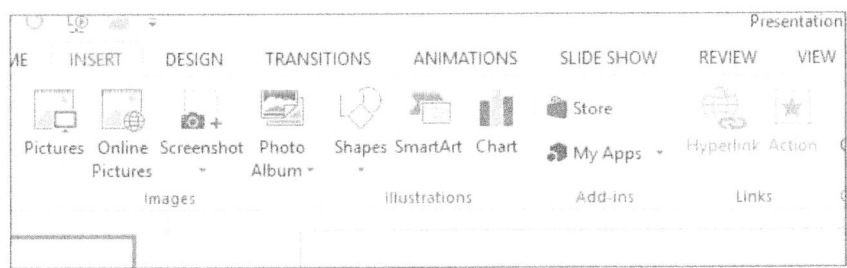

3) **Design**

On the Design tab, you can format the slide background, add a theme or color scheme.

POWERPOINT FOR DUMMIES

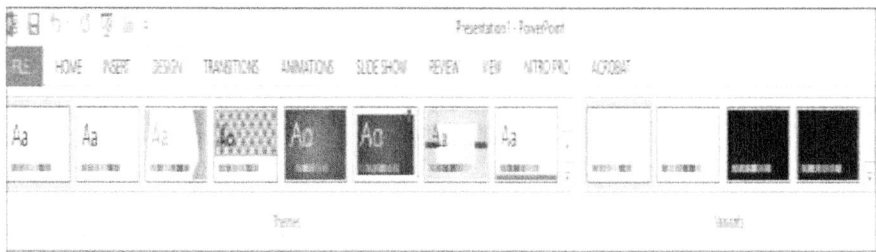

4) Transition

The transition tab gives several options to choose how you want your slice to change from one to the next

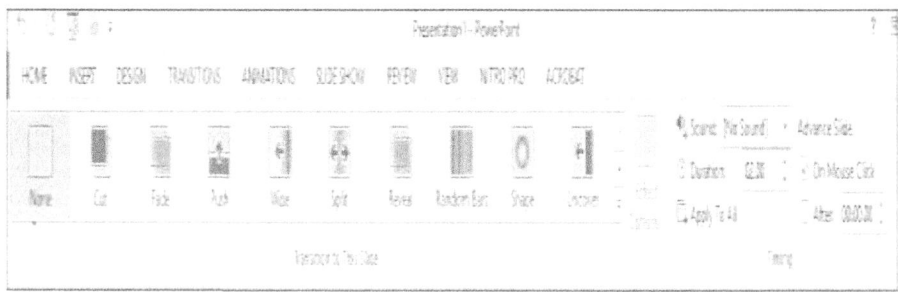

5) Animation

The animation tab gives you the freedom to arrange the movement of things in your slide. There are many options on display and if they do not satisfy you, you can click the more icon.

POWERPOINT FOR DUMMIES

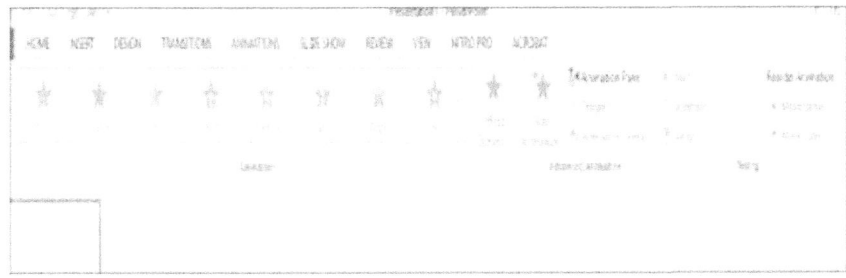

6) **Slideshows**

In the slide show tab, you can set up the way you want others to see your presentation

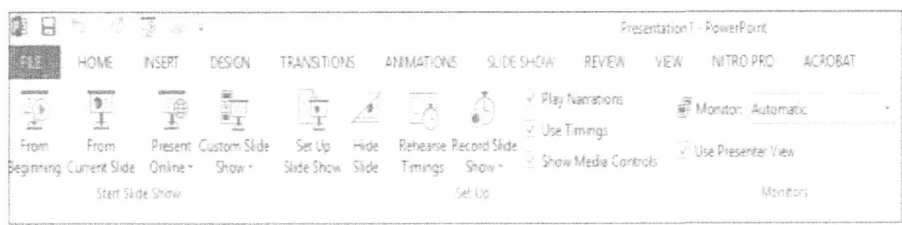

7) **Review**

In the review tab, there are options to add comments and compare a presentation with a previously saved one.

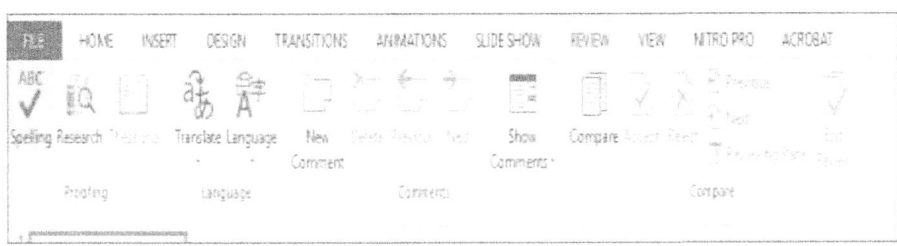

POWERPOINT FOR DUMMIES

8) View

On this tab, you will look at your presentation in diverse ways, based on the point you are in the creation process.

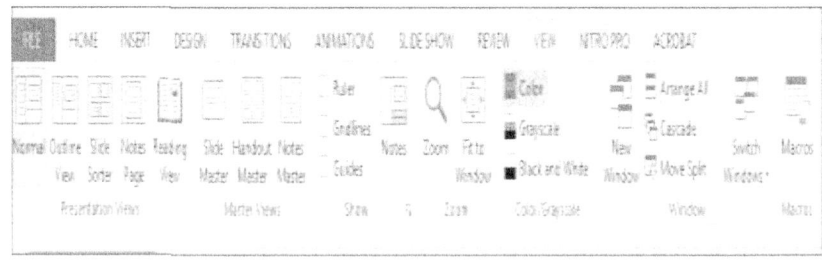

9) File

This tab is located at the end of the ribbon and is used for working on a file. Activities like opening, saving, printing, and more can be done on this tab.

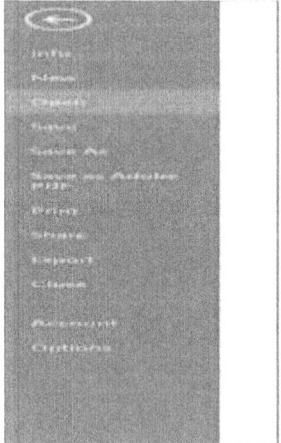

Working in the backstage view

After your PowerPoint is up and running, you can create a presentation in a backstage view by tapping on the file tab to switch to the backstage view and click the new command. This makes a list of ways to create a presentation. Which includes: creating a presentation, opening a presentation, saving a presentation, and so on.

The Backstage view gives you access to access to save, and open information about the file currently opened. It also helps in creating a new file, printing, and viewing recent files that you open. It provides additional information such as the file size, creation date, last changed date,. Talking about the behind scene stuff.

To create a presentation in backstage view

- Click the file tab, this will take you to the backstage view.
- Click New, you will find this on the left side of the window.
- Click the Blank presentation.

In creating a new presentation, you would need a template. You might wonder what a template is. A template is a pre-designed presentation. The primary purpose of a template is to help create a slide in no time. It often includes designs, custom formatting, etc. It is just to help you save time in starting a new project

To choose a template go to the search bar to find something that suits you. All you have to do is fill in your keyword.

Opening an existing presentation

Apart from creating a new presentation, you may need to open a presentation that was saved before. To do that:

- Click the file tab
- Scroll to the open option and click it.

Saving Presentation:

Click the save command on the toolbar

If you are saving for the first time the "Save As" option will pop up in the backstage view You will have to pick a location where you save and also give it a name.

If you wish to save the presentation in another version while keeping the original. All you have to do is click the "save as" option and follow the prompts.

You can also use the backstage view to share a presentation, pin a presentation, and a lot more. There are lots of things to explore there.

Views in PowerPoints and their uses

There are different views in PowerPoint with each having its peculiarity.

Creation and Editing Views

1) **Normal View**

    The normal view is the editing view. The writing and designing of the presentation happen here. In this view there are 3 working areas:

    - On the right side, there is a slide pane displaying a clear view of the present slide.
    - On the left side, there is a Thumbnail pane. It is an alternating tab in between the outline of slide text and the slide displayed as thumbnails.
    - On the bottom, you will find the note pane.

2) **Slide sorter view**

    The slide sorter gives you the overall view of the presentation after you are done with the creation and editing of your presentation. In this view it is easier to reorder, add, and delete slides, check out your animation effects and preview your transition.

    It is a view of all slides in thumbnail form.

3) **Outline View**

In this view, you have your presentation displayed as an outline. The main text and titles make up the outline on each side. On the left side of the pane appears the title of each slide, the slide icon and number also appears here. This view gives you an overview of your presentation and makes it easy for you to do general editing on your presentation.

4) **Notes Page View**

Located under the slide pane, you can easily type notes that apply to the presentation slides. You can put these notes in your online presence that you send to your audience or print them out to your audience.

5) **Master Views**

These are the major slides storing the information such as the theme colors, theme fonts, theme effects, background, and every other vital information about the presentation.

This view includes Notes, Handouts, and Slide views.

The major advantage of working in this view is that it is easier to make general changes to every slide and notes in your presentation.

Presentation Views

1) **Slide Show view**

    In this view, you see exactly how your presentation will look to the audience. The timing, animation effects, graphics will appear as it will be in the actual show. Your slides will fill up the full screen.

2) **Presenter View**

    In this view, you can manage your slides even while you are presenting. It helps you track how much time you've spent and display notes that are visible to only you and so on.

Printing your Presentation.

1) **Print Preview**

    This view gives you the flexibility to tweak the settings to how you want it.

2) **Slide Sorter View**

    As explained earlier this view leaves your presentation in thumbnail form making it easy to rearrange and sort your slides.

Chapter 2

Understanding Slide Layouts, Themes, and Placeholders

The slide layouts comprise of the positioning, formatting, and the place holders boxes for every content appearing in a slide. Additionally, slide layouts contain the slides effects,colors, theme elements, and fonts. There is an inbuilt slide layout that you can tweak to your satisfaction based on needs. You can also share your custom layout with others who also create their presentation on PowerPoint.

POWERPOINT FOR DUMMIES

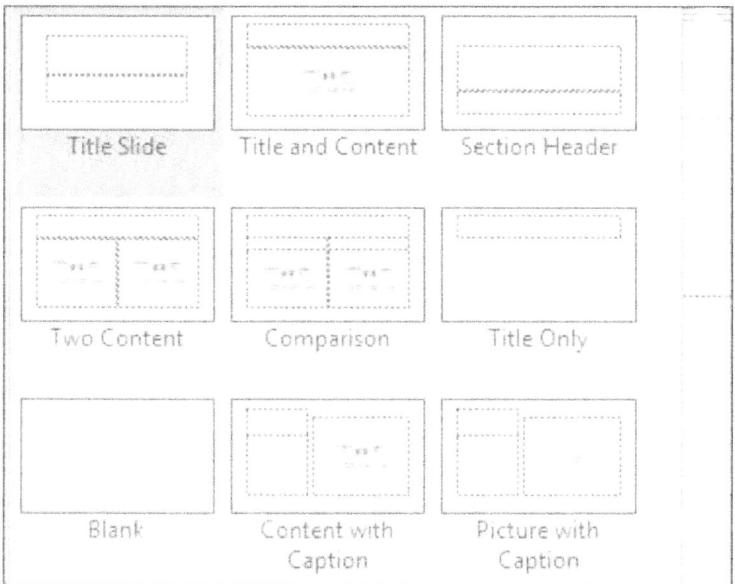

Image 2.1: PowerPoint standard slide layout, showing the placement of different placeholders for graphics or text

You can modify the inbuilt PowerPoint standard slide layouts in the Slide Master view.

Types of Slide layout

- **Title and Content**: This layout is the default slide layout and the most commonly used slide layout.
- **Title Slide**: You can use this slide layout at the start of your presentation to present your topics.

- **Section Header**: You use this for the separation of the different sections of a presentation.
- **Two Content**: As the name implies, use this slide layout to show two columns containing graphic and text content.
- **Comparison**: This slide can compare two types of the same contents, for instance, two different tables. It looks like the Two Content Layout. The difference is that there is a heading text box over each of the content.
- **Title Only**: Make use of this layout if you intend to place only a title on the page instead of a title and subtitle. It leaves the area beneath the title empty for the addition of other content (such as tables, charts, or pictures).
- **Blank**: You use this when a picture or other graphic object needs no extra information.
- **Content with Caption**: as the name implies has two columns for text and content. The left column is the placeholders for text. And the right column, the placeholders for images and illustrations.

Where do you find slide layouts?

If you wish to use a designed layout for a specific slide, click on the slide. After that, go to the tool ribbon and click on the home tab, click the layout option, and choose the structure you want from the options appearing in the gallery.

POWERPOINT FOR DUMMIES

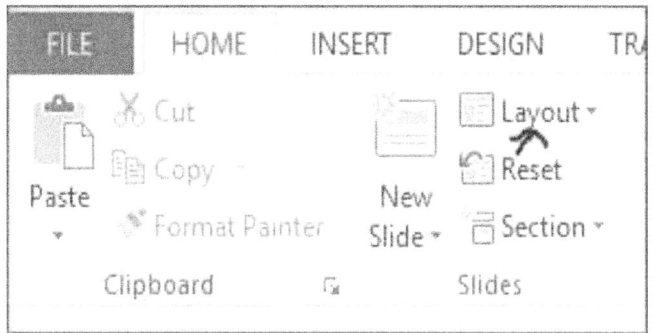

You can customize your slide layouts in the master view. As explained before, the layout master shows as a thumbnail in the thumbnail pane under the slide master. Tap a layout master in the thumbnail and start customizing

If you wish to customize a slide layout definition that you will later apply to individual slides. Go to the toolbar label, click view, and then slide master. However, you can't get this feature on PowerPoint for the web.

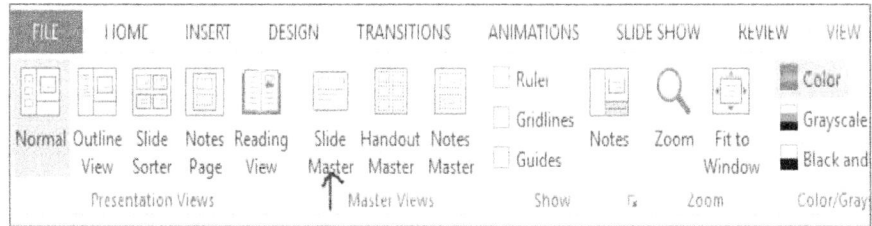

Applying a slide layout

Put in order the slide content with carrying slide layouts to suit your preference or to make it clearer and easier to read. Then do the following:

- Click on the slide you intend to change the layout for.
- Click home and then layout
- Click the layout that you desire

TIP: If at all, you changed a layout, and you don't like it, and you want it to return to the initial design. All you have to do is click home and then reset, making use of

The layout comprises placeholders for videos, shapes, pictures, formatting, and more. It also encompasses the proper configuration for the objects, things like background, colors, effects, and fonts.

Editing and Reapplying Slides

If, after applying a slide layout to a slide or two in your presentation, you also went back to edit that layout by adding a prompt text,

POWERPOINT FOR DUMMIES

adding a placeholder, or any action that can alter the structure. Reapply the layout to the slides so that the slides conform to the updated layout. Here explains how you can change and rename a layout.

Changing an existing layout

1) Go to the View label, tap Slide Master.
2) Go to the section of the thumbnail containing the slide masters and layouts and pick the structure that has the most similar placeholder arrangements to your desired slide look.

TIP: Remember, the top thumbnail is always the slide master, and the other slide layout will always be below it.

POWERPOINT FOR DUMMIES

> Click to edit Master title style
> - Click to edit Master text styles
>   - Second level
>   - Third level
>   - Fourth level
>   - Fifth level

3) For you to alter an existing layout, do the following
- Add, edit, or remove a placeholder on a slide layout.
- To add a placeholder: Go to the Slide Master tab, and select Insert Placeholder, and choose a placeholder type from the list.
- Select a location on the layout and drag to draw the placeholder. (more will be discussed placeholders later)

Renaming Layout

If you want to give a layout another name,
- Go to the layout thumbnail list,

- Right-click the design you want and tap the rename layout option.
- In the dialog box for layout renaming, fill in a new name that fits the layout you just created and click on Rename.

After doing this, go to the slide master tab and close the master view

Applying Updates

To make your changes come into effect, apply the updates so they can come into effects. To do this:
- Go to the Normal View.
- Under the thumbnail section, tap the slide you want the updated layout to be reapplied to.

Tip: If you want to choose more than one slide, hold down the control key and click on the slides you wish to.

2) Go to the Home tab in the Slides group, click Layout, and pick the design you have updated in the slide master view.

What are themes?

Themes are pre-designed set of fonts, visual effects and colors to give your slide a uniform and professional look. The application of themes gives that uniform look to your slide with less stress involved. For instance,

- Light-colored text on a background and the other way round, just to make reading easy
- When an image or a chart is added to a slide, a color that will suit the other theme elements will be applied by PowerPoint.

Here is an example of three different themes used on a slide:

POWERPOINT FOR DUMMIES

Choosing a theme for your presentation

On PowerPoint, there are a lot of preset themes. You can find them on the Ribbon's design tab. To choose a theme:

- Open a slide, go to the design tab, and place your cursor on a theme- this will let you get a preview of how it would influence your slides to look.
- Click the more icon to have a view of the complete theme gallery.

POWERPOINT FOR DUMMIES

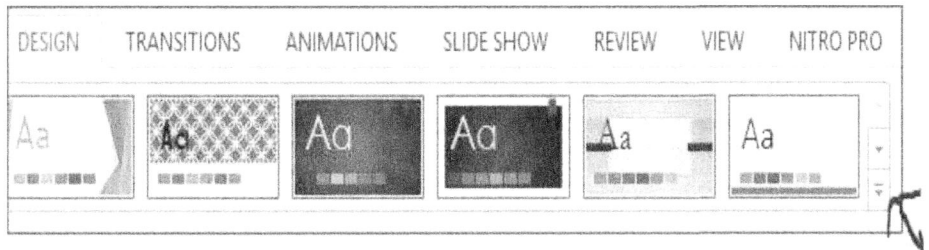

- After finding a suitable theme, click the thumbnail to apply the theme every slides in your presentation.

Using multiple themes in a presentation

If you already have a theme in your presentation but you wish to add more, there is a way to go about it. To add a second theme or another slide Master that has a different theme to your presentation, do the following.

- Go to the view tab and click on the slide master

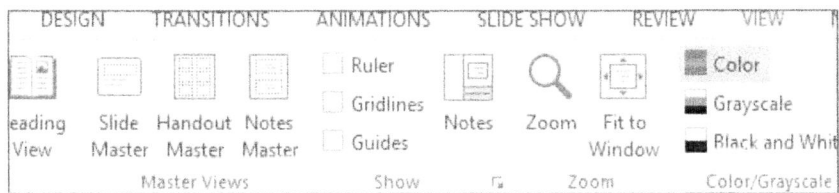

- On the Slide Master tab, click insert slide master
  You will have a second slide master inserted in the left thumbnail pane
- Now that the new slide master has been selected in the thumbnail pane

Go to the slide master tab of the ribbon, select themes, and pick the themes you want from the list.

POWERPOINT FOR DUMMIES

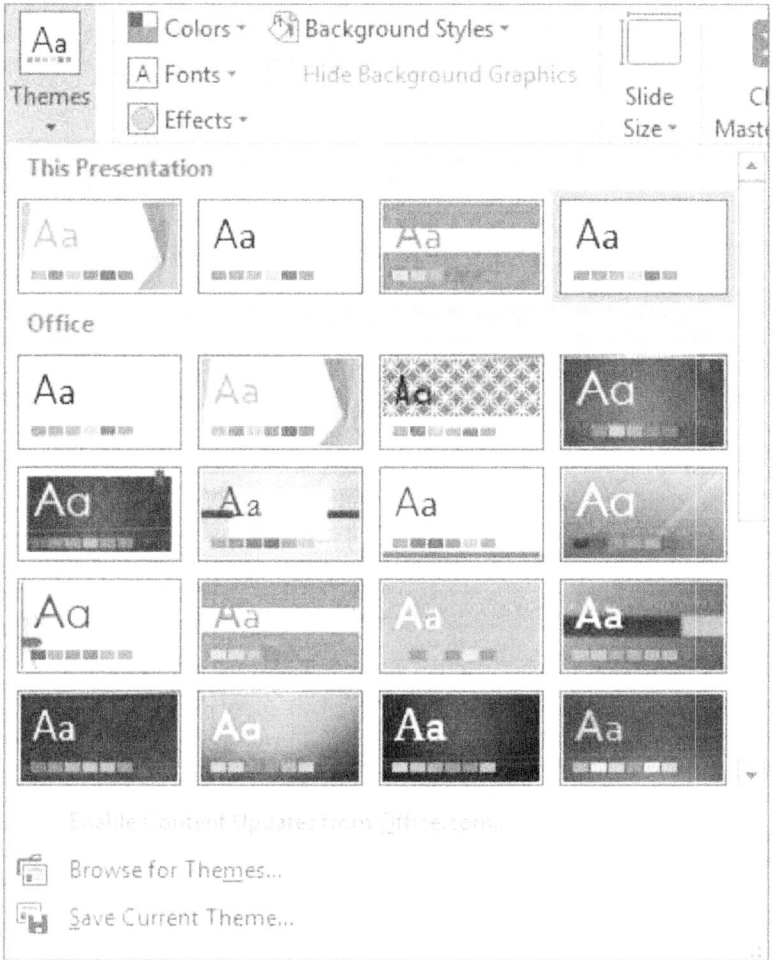

The newly added Slide Master will now have a different theme from the other Slide Master in your presentation.

- After the selections, click close Master view.

Note: The newly selected hasn't been applied yet to any slide. Remember, you now have two different themes. To make use of both themes follow these procedures.

To apply themes to your slides:
    1) Apply a theme to a new slide:
- Click the slide you wish to change.
- Beneath the slides, tap the down arrow next to the Layout to reveal an option of thumbnails
- Scroll the thumbnails and pick the one you want.

POWERPOINT FOR DUMMIES

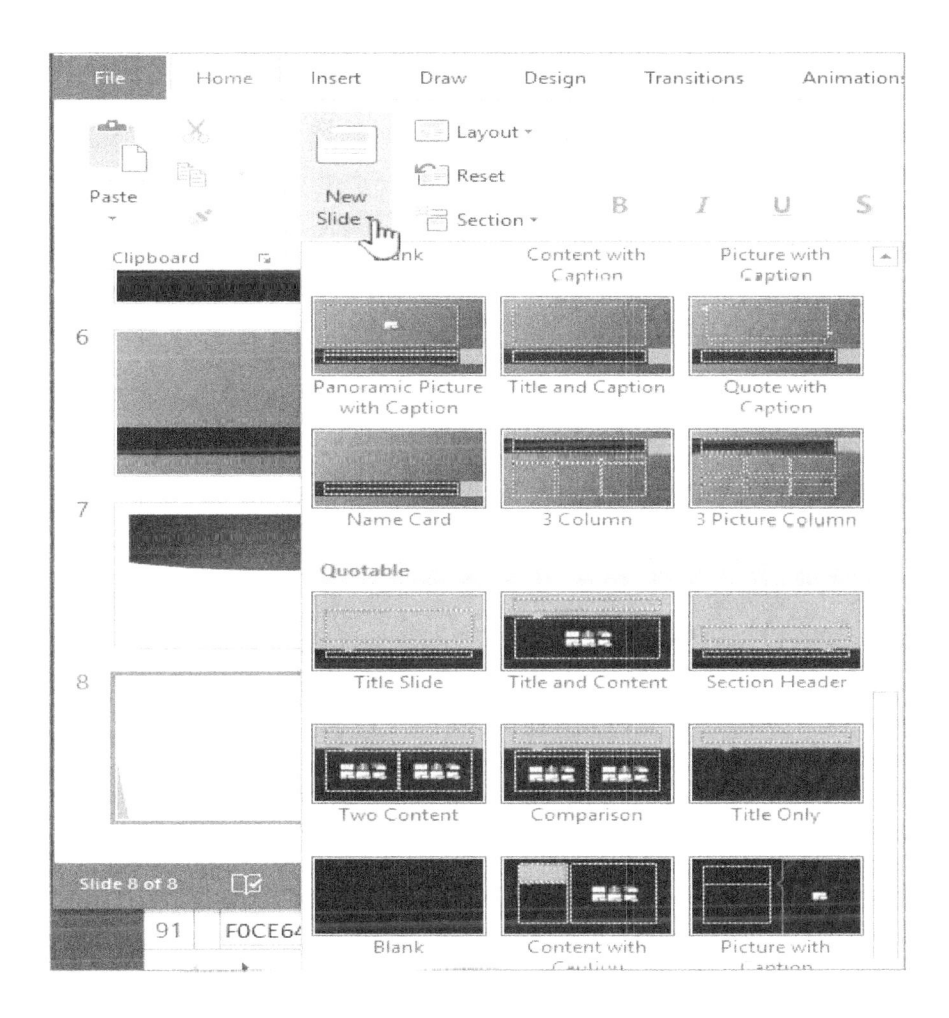

Apply a theme to existing slides.

- Click the slide you want to customize.

- Under Slides, click the down arrow next to Layout to drop down a selection of thumbnails.

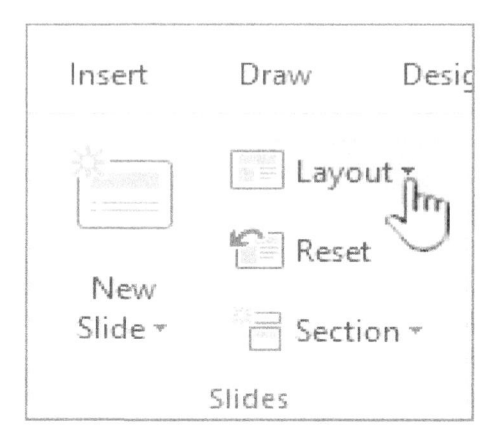

- Beneath the slides, click the down arrow (the one next to layout) to drop down an option of thumbnails
- Go through the thumbnails and select the theme you want to use

Creating themes in PowerPoint

Sometimes you may not be satisfied with theme available and might want to build your custom theme. To create a custom theme you have to start with an inbuilt office theme. After which can customize it by altering any of the fonts, colors or effects. The changing of the themes effects, fonts, colors and save of settings will be described below.

Changing theme colors

There are four texts, six accent colors, two hyperlink colors and four background colors in the theme colors. Under sample section, you can view how the colors and font styles will look before you decide on which color to combine together. To change your theme

- Go to the design tab and click on the variants group.
- Click the drop down arrow- this opens the color variants gallery.
- Click colors and select customize colors. The Create New theme section comes up.
- Under Create New Theme Colors section, select Theme colors, and do these
- Click the button beside the theme color elements name (for instance Hyperlink, background) that you want to work on. Go to theme colors and select a color.

-Or-

Do either of these

1) Click more colors and do either of these:
2) Type the name of the new theme colors combination in the Name box and click save
    - Go to the standard tab and chose a color.

POWERPOINT FOR DUMMIES

- Go to the custom tab enter the formula number of the color you want
- Do the same for the theme color element you want to customize.

After defining a custom color scheme, it will be on colors drop menu

TIP

To revert all theme color elements to their original theme colors, click Reset before saving.

Changing theme fonts

If you change the fonts of your themes all the title and bullet text in the presentation will be updated.

- Go to the view tab and click the Slide Master.
- In the slide master click Fonts and then customize fonts.
- Under the Create New Theme fonts section, go to the heading fonts and Body font boxes choose the font you want.
- Type the name of the new theme fonts in the Name box and select save

Choose a set of theme effects

There are various theme effects such as reflections, fills, shadows, lines and more. Although you cannot create your own set of theme effects, you can select a set of effects that suits your presentation.
- Go to the view tab and click Slide Master.
- Under the slide master tab, click effects.
- Choose the set of effects you want.

Save a theme

To apply your new theme to other presentations you have to save the changes made to your fonts, colors and effects as a theme.

- Go to the view tab and click Slide Master.
- Under Slide Master Tab click Themes.
- Select save current theme.
- Type the name for the theme in the file name box and click save.

Note: the new theme will be saved as a .thmx file in your Local drive Document themes folder. Also the new theme will be added automatically to the custom themes group on the design tab.

What is a PowerPoint template?

Many people mix up the definition of template and design. A template is a combination of a theme and some content for a particular PURPOSE. The purpose might be a business plan, lecturer's presentation, etc. A template has theme elements that work together - fonts, backgrounds, effects, etc., and content you come up with to present your ideas.

There are different free templates that you can apply in your PowerPoint presentation on Templates.office.com

Still not satisfied? You can also create and save your custom template. You can reuse them and also share with others.

Using Placeholders

What are Placeholders?

Placeholders are pre-designed containers on a slide for displaying content such as graphics, text, pictures, tables, movies. They can be edited, moved, and resized. PowerPoint displays placeholders as a rectangular box with dots and you will find them in an inbuilt slide. The essence is to make formatting easy.

Formatting a placeholder happens in the slide master. After which you add content to it in the Normal view

Changing the Prompt text of a placeholder.

- You can change the (click to edit) prompt text for a placeholder
- Go to the View label, under the master views group, select slide master.
- In the thumbnail, pane pick the layout you wish to effect change
- On the layout tab in the main pane, click the prompt text and type the text you wish to use to replace it.

After completing the changes in slide master view, click close master view to return to normal view

Resizing or repositioning a placeholder

- Go to the View tab, and select Slide Master
- On the slide layout you wish to change, tap the placeholder you intend to work on and do either of these:
- If you want to its size, point your cursor to one of the sizing handles. Once the cursor becomes a two-headed arrow, drag the handle
- For repositioning, point your cursor to one I of the borders. Once the arrow turns to a four-headed arrow, drag the placeholder to the new position.
- Go to the Slide Master tab, and Close the Master View.
- Go to the thumbnail pane, in the normal view, select all the slides that use the slide layout you just changed

TIP: If you want to select multiple slides, press and hold down the Ctrl Key. Then click each slide.

- Go to the home tab click layout and pick the layout containing the revised placeholders. Doing this will finalize the changes made to the placeholder by reapplying the revised slide layout to an actual slide.

Types of Layout

Adding a placeholder to a slide layout

You can only add placeholders to slide layouts and not the individual slides in the presentation.

- On the View tab, click Slide Master.
- Go to the view tab and click the slide master
- In the left thumbnail pane, click the slide layout that you want to add one or more placeholders.
- Go to the Slide Master tab, click insert placeholder, and pick the kind of placeholder that you wish to add.

POWERPOINT FOR DUMMIES

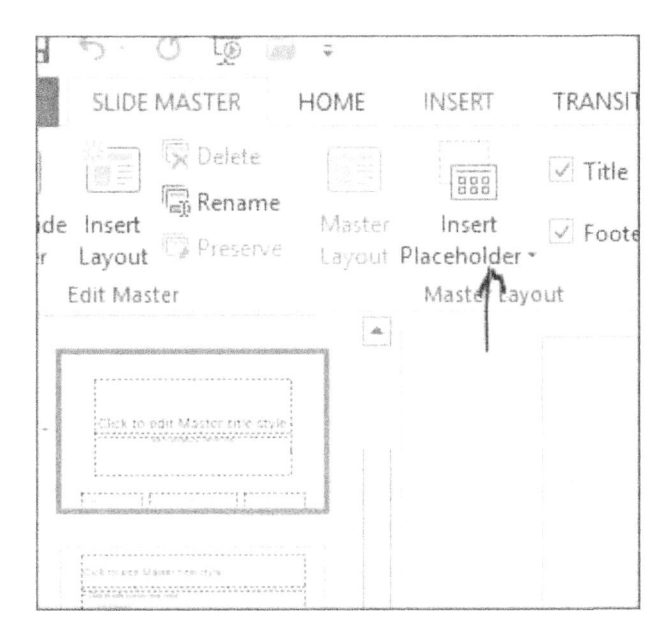

- Click a location on the slide layout, and then drag to draw the placeholder. You can add as many placeholders as you like.
- If you add a text placeholder, you can customize the prompt text ("Click to edit ...") that appears in it:
- After adding a text placeholder you can change the prompt text that appears in it
- Select the default text in the placeholder, and replace it with your prompt text.
- Click the initial text in the placeholder, and replace it with your customized prompt text.

Switch to the Home tab to format the prompt text as you want it to appear.

- Go to the Home tab to format the prompt text just as you would like it to appear.
- Now that you have selected the text, you can now change the font or font size.
- If any bullet appears before your default prompt text and you do not want it, go to the paragraph group, tap the down arrow next to bullets and select none.
- When you're done, on the Slide Master tab, click Close Master View.
- If you are through with the process, go to the Slide Master tab and click close Master view
- In Normal View, go to the thumbnail pane, select all the slides you used in the slide layout you just changed.

Tip: for multiple slide selection, press down the Ctrl key and click each slide

Go to the home tab, click Layout, and select the layout that has the revised placeholders.

Doing this will help complete the placeholder change by reapplying the revised layout to an actual slide.

Removing a placeholder

POWERPOINT FOR DUMMIES

It is best if you don't remove a placeholder from a pre-built slide layout. If at all you wish to make any changes, duplicate the layout, give it a unique name, and edit that copy.

- Go to the View tab, and select Slide Master.
- Go to the left thumbnail pane, click the slide layout that you wish to change.
- Select the placeholder on the layout, then press the Delete key.
- Click the placeholder on the layout and click the delete key.

Working with Objects

The simplest way to move around on your presentation in PowerPoint is by using your Page up and Page down keys. Press the page up key to move backward to the previous slide and Page down to move to the next slide. Alternatively, you can make use of the vertical scroll bar on the right side of the screen to move around your presentation.

The scroll box is another quick means of moving from slide to slide in your presentation. Just drag the scroll bar in an upward-downward movement. A small tooltip comes up when you drag the scroll bar- this is to tell you the slide that will be displayed if you stop dragging at that point.

You can make use of Single-headed and double-headed arrows. Clicking and holding the single-headed arrow (at the top or bottom of the vertical scroll bar) enables you to move backward and forward.

In like fashion you can move backward and forward by clicking the double-headed arrow at the bottom of the scroll bar. If your PC has the touchscreen feature, you can from side to side with just a flick of your finger.

Selection of Objects

To select objects you have to be in the Normal view, remember normal view is the editing mode. You can select slides in the slide sorter view but not the objects in it. Scroll over and click the text you want to edit. A box pops up immediately around the object and you see a text insertion point come up, you can start typing.

To work on other types of objects differs from working on the text object. Click on the object to select it, you would see a rectangular object pop up- this is to tell you that the object is now hooked. After that, you can move the object around, or resize the object.

Tip: To select more than one object, click the first object. Hold the Ctrl key down while selecting other objects you want to add.

You can also make use of the tab key to select an object. Press the tab key this selects this first object on the slide. Press it again to select the next, again to select the next and it goes on like that until you get the object, you want to select.

The tab key can come in handy during work especially when you find it difficult to point to the participants' object you intend to select- this occurs mostly when the desired objects are hidden under another object.

Working on Text Objects

Once a text is highlighted for editing, PowerPoint converts into a mini word processor to allow for editing. PowerPoint often formats text in bullets character at the start of each paragraph. However, you can change the bullet character if you aren't satisfied with the default bullet character.

Moving around a text object: you can move around by making use of the arrow keys or with the use of a mouse. Additionally, you can make use of the home and end keys to move the point of insertion to the end and start of the line you're working on. Furthermore, you can make use of the arrow keys with the Ctrl keys to navigate around more easily. For instance, if you use the Ctrl key and the right arrow key you'll have the entire text moved to the right at a time.

To delete a text just press the Backspace or delete keys. You can also delete from the point of Insertion by making use of the Ctrl key + the delete key.

Selection of Text.

There is some editing operation that will require that you highlight or select the text on which you want to work on. Here are ways to select lines of text:

- With the use of Mouse: move your cursor to the start of the text you want to highlight, click, and drag over the text. Once you have covered the text you want, release the mouse.
- With the use of Keyboard: press the Shift key down + the arrow key to move to the point of insertion.

There is an automatic word selection feature that tries to preempt your thoughts when you highlight a text. If you dislike this feature, you can have it disabled in the backstage view. Here are tricks to select different amounts of text:

- Move the cursor to anywhere in the word and double click.
- For an entire paragraph: move the cursor anywhere in the paragraph and click thrice.

After this, you can delete, replace, cut, copy, paste the text, and do whatever you want to do with the text.

Chapter 3

Slides

The title slide is the only slide that pops up after you create a presentation from a design template. At this point, you can add more Slides to create the kind of presentation you want. You might import Slides from other presentations or create Slides that will fit the kind of content you want to create.

If the presentation you're working on will require multiple slides, you can arrange them into sections. However, the audience will not see these sections but it makes it easier to work with slide content in logical segments. An overall constant look, logical presentation with the right variations at the right places will make it easier for your audience to understand the idea you're conveying accurately. In this section you'll be exposed to the procedures involved in the addition and deleting of slides, rearranging sections and slides, segmenting the presentation into sections, and changing slides background.

Addition and Removal of Slides

How a slide appears and how the structure is, is defined by the slide layouts associated with the Slide master, which is a part of the design template. Elements of slides such as- the text box locations, sizes and formats, Standard headers or footers, slide background and graphics, default paragraph, and character format are all controlled by the **Slide Layout.**

The slide master can only have one slide layout, but they mostly have unique layouts for the slide displaying the presentation title, section titles, and different combinations of slide content and title, and an empty slide made up of the only background.

As discussed in the previous section there are different slide layouts. Each bearing a name that suggests its primary application, but the truth is you aren't limited to the name suggestion. You can input any content and change the layout of any slide. You'll always see the slide layout available in the new slide tab

Inserting New Slide

After you create a new slide, PowerPoint will automatically place it after the active side at the point. Also, because of the standard PowerPoint template, any slide added after a slide other than the title slide will have a layout of the preceding slide.

If you intend to use a different layout, you can choose the layout you want when you insert the slide. Alternatively, you can also change the layout of the slide after you create the slide. Let's look at different ways of adding slides.

Adding a slide based on the default slide layout.
- Click the new Slide you intend to add the new slide after.

POWERPOINT FOR DUMMIES

- Go to the home tab
- In the slides section, click on the New slide button

Tip: you can use the Ctrl + M key on your keyboard to make this faster.

To add a slide based on a different slide layout

- Click the slide you want the newly added slide to appear after.
- Go to the home tab. In the Slide section.
- Click the new slide **arrow-** this will make the New slide gallery and menu pop up
- In the slide gallery, select the thumbnail of the slide layout to add a slide based on that layout.

Copying and importation of slides and content

You can make use of the slides from a previous presentation, this can be done in two ways-

1. By copying the slides from the original presentation and pasting it in the new presentation.
2. You can use the Slide tool again- this showcases the content of the original presentation and gives you the chance to select the slides you want to insert in the new presentation.

Duplicating Slides

You can make a copy of an existing slide to reuse it as the basis for a new Slide. If you wish, you can modify the copied slide Instead of going through the stress of creating from the scratch. To insert a copy of a slide immediately following the original slide

Make sure the presentation is in Normal view- remember this is the editing view.

- Go to the thumbnails pane
- Right-click the slide you want to create a copy of
- Click duplicate slide

To insert a copy of one or more slides anywhere in a presentation put the presentation in the Normal or Slide Sorter View and do either of these two

1. Go to the home tab In the Clipboard group
- Tap the copy button.
- Choose the slide thumbnail and select Copy

OR

2. Click the side thumbnail (or thumbnails if more than one)
- Press the Ctrl +C keys

Now you have the slide copied to insert it, do the following:
1. Select the thumbnail you want to insert the copy (or copies) after. Alternatively, you can click the space after the thumbnail.

POWERPOINT FOR DUMMIES

2. On the Home tab, go to the clipboard board group, click the paste option Or press the Ctrl + V keys
3. Right-click where you intend to insert the slide copy
4. A paste option would pop up, in the shortcut menu select the keep source formatting option

To add extra copies repeat the number 3 process

Importing Slides

If there are certain slides, you use them repeatedly in your presentations. For instance an introductory slide, you do not always have to create from the scratch for each presentation. You can easily make use of a slide from one presentation in another presentation.

NOTE: You can make use of the same method to reuse a slide from another person's presentation to standardize the structure and appearance of the slide content with other members of your organization.

The new slide will take on the formatting of the new presentation except you modify it.

If the content of your presentation is in a document, you can modify the content in the outline format, after which you can import the outline into PowerPoint. For you to do this you have to format the content of the document you wish to import into headings.

PowerPoint has been designed to change some style into a heading, it will change some into bulleted characters while some will be completely ignored. This is how it works, the Title, Subtitle, Heading 1, any bulleted character or any numbered list level will be converted into Slide title. Also, Headings 2, Headings 3 up to Headings 9 will be converted to First level bulleted list, second-level bulleted list, and the corresponding number respectively.

To insert a slide from another presentation

There are 3 different ways to insert a slide from another presentation.

Method 1

- Let the presentation be in the Normal View.
- Go to the home or Insert tab. In the slide group, select the New Slide Arrow
- Beneath the gallery is the new slide menu
- Select the Reuse slide option- this makes the Reuse pane pop up on the right side of the screen.

- Tap the browse button and select the browse file. Browse the file that contains the presentation you want to insert. Once you find it, double click the presentation.

PowerPoint will create copies of the slide. Also, the destination themes will apply to the copies.

Method 2
- Tap the browse icon
- Click Browse slide Library
- Browse to the slide Library containing the slide or slides you want to use. The Reuse section displays the available slides thumbnails
- In the Reuse slide section, select the slide or slides thumbnail that you want to add to your presentation
- Close the Reuse Slides section.

NOTE: The reused slides will take the design of the new presentation it is inserted in. If you still want the slide to keep the formatting of the source presentation, click the Source formatting option at the end of the Reuse pane

Method 3
- Open the source and destination presentations in PowerPoint.

POWERPOINT FOR DUMMIES

- Put each presentation in the Normal or Sorter View.
- Display each presentation in Normal view or Slide Sorter view.
- Display the two PowerPoint windows side by side.
- In the source presentation, click the slide or slides you intend to copy.
- Drag your selections to the destination presentation.

You would see a horizontal line pop up between the slide thumbnails in the Normal view or a vertical line pop up between the Slide thumbnails- this is to indicate the point at which PowerPoint will insert the slides.

Extra

If the presentation you want to import slides from is one in which you've been previously connected. Just click the down arrow in the Insert Slide- this expands the list.
Select the presentation filename in the Open tab of the Reuse Slide Section.

Preparing a source document for importation to a presentation
- Create the content you want to be displayed on the slides (it could be a word or anything you wish to add) in a document.

POWERPOINT FOR DUMMIES

- Check the styles you apply to the content you want to add to the presentation. The title, subtitle, heading 1, heading 2 up to Heading 9 will be converted to slide titles as discussed earlier. Save and close the document.

Creating a presentation by importing a Word document.

- Go to the backstage view, on the open page click browse.
- You would see different file types in the file type list. Click all files.
- Look for the folder containing the slide title and bullet character information.
- Double-tap the document to create a new presentation.
- Choose all the slides in the new presentation.
- Go to the home tab in the Slide group tap the reset button.
- Choose the design template you want and click apply.

Creating slides in Existing presentation by the importation of Word Documents

- Select the slide you want your new slide to appear after.
- Go to the Home tab or Insert tab
- Click on the slide group and tap the new slide arrow.
- The New slide menu will drop, under the gallery, select slides from an outline- this makes the Insert Outline dialog box to open

- Browse for the folder containing the word document you intend to use for the Slide titles and content.
- Double-tap the document to insert slides based on its content.

Hide and delete slides

If after creating a slide you don't like the output or you feel it is unnecessary, you can delete it. Also, if you don't need a particular slide at a time but feel it might be useful later on, you can hide it

If you create a slide and then later realize that you don't need it, you can delete it. If you don't need the slide for a presentation to a specific audience but might need it later, you can hide the slide instead. PowerPoint will not display hidden slides in the slide show but will remain available in the thumbnails pane. However, their thumbnails will be dimmed and their slide crossed with a backslash symbol (\).

To delete slides

Method 1

- Right-click a single slide and then click Delete Slide.
- Right-click the slide you wish to delete. Select the Delete Slide options.

Method 2

Select the slide or slides you want to delete.

Do any of the following:

- Right-click the selection and then click Delete Slide. Or
- On the Home tab, in the Clipboard group, click Cut.
- Press the Delete key.

For multiple slides

- Press and hold down the Ctrl key.
- Move to the left thumbnail pane and select the slides.
- Release the Ctrl key after you are through with the selections.
- Right-click the selected slides and click delete from the options that appear.

If it is a sequence of slides

- Press and hold the shift key down.
- Click the first and last slide of the sequence.
- Release the Shift key, right-click the selected slide and click delete

💡

PowerPoint renumbers all subsequent slides when you add or delete slides.

Hiding Slides

Click the Slide or Slides you wish to work on and do any of these two.

1. Right-click the selected slides then select the Hide option.
2. Go to the slide show tab.
    - Click the setup group and select the Hide button.

Rearranging the order of slides

- In the section on the left
- select the thumbnail of the slide you want to move
- Drag it to the new position you want.

Selecting multiple slides.

- Hold down the Ctrl key.
- On the left section click the slides you wish to move.
- Release the Ctrl key
- Drag the Slide to the new position

-

Chapter 4

Writing and Formatting Text

You can add text to a slide by typing right inside the box or by adding a text box. After which we can format the text accordingly. Formatting to be discussed in the next section. Furthermore, text can be added to shapes and Placeholders.

Let's move on to the various ways you can add text to a slide:

Adding Text to a Placeholder

To do this, follow the steps listed below:

- Just click the inside of the placeholder.
- Type your text into it or paste previously copied text.

Tip: PowerPoint will reduce the text size if it goes beyond the placeholder's size- this is to make the text fit in.

Below, the dotted border represents the placeholder that contains the title text for the slide.

To add a text that can be edited by anyone to text box

- Go to the normal view.
- Click the inside of the text box.

POWERPOINT FOR DUMMIES

- Type into the box or paste a previously copied text

To insert into a text box, texts that cannot be edited and is permanent.

- Go to the Slide Master view.
- Click the inside of the text box.
- Type the text into or paste it

You can use the text boxes to input text at any point on a slide. All you have to do is create a text box around the point

Adding Text to a Shape

It is possible to add text to shapes such as circles, rectangles, squares. After inputting a text into a shape, it becomes attached to it and will move and rotate with it.

To Insert text to a shape.

- Click the shape
- Type in or paste your text.

Texts added in normal view are editable by anyone but texts added in Slide master are permanent and can't be edited.

Formatting

There are pre-designed templates in PowerPoint as discussed earlier and these templates include fonts, font sizes, colors, and other formatting. You may want to garnish your presentation and make it more stylish therefore needing to change these preset themes. Here are some things you can do to enhance your presentation:

- **Changing a Font with another**: because of preference you might prefer a font over the other and might desire to change it. However, apply caution and ensure everyone can read your presentation. Don't be too creative especially if the presentation is for a formal gathering, for instance, a business presentation.

- **Changing Font Size**:

    Ever looked at a book and you find it difficult to read because the font is too small or reading becomes difficult because of ridiculously big fonts. That must have happened to you before. So if you feel dissatisfied with the font size of your presentation you can change it. For instance, if your title is too long and won't fit in one line, you might want to reduce the font size. Another scenario is a situation where you have just a few bullet points you might increase the font size to fill the page. However, make sure the font size is appropriate for the presentation. Make sure the texts are readable

- **Bold, Italics, Color**- This is mostly for emphasis, maybe you want your audience to take note of an important point.

You can either add color to the text, make it bold, put it in Italics, or even have it underlined.

Moving forward to the text formatting operations that can be done within PowerPoint, but before that let's look at ways you can Format. There are two ways to go about it:

1) Making use of the Font dialog box to make a series of changes in one place and to put in the default font.
2) Applying text formatting on each text by making use of the buttons in the formatting toolbar.

Using the Font Dialog Box

To make use of the Font dialog box for text formatting. Do the following:

1. Highlight the text you plan to format and choose format, font. The font dialog will come up.
2. Choose the Font that you would like to use from the font list. Scroll down the list for extra font selections.
3. Pick a font style: Regular, Italic, Bold, or Bold Italic
4. Select a color from the arrays of the color displayed by the Color list. If you want extra color choices, click the more icon to open the colors dialog box.
5. Pick a Size: Select a preset size or input an exact size in the edit box.

6. You can get the additional effect by looking at the check box next to the following:

- **Underline**: this will underline the highlighted text.
- Emboss: this will create an embossed effect on the highlighted text. Superscript: this will increase the text above the baseline and decrease the font size. It adjusts the Offset to 30%, although you can change it.
- **Subscript**: this will decrease the text below the standard and also decrease the font size. Adjusts the Offset to 25%, although like superscript this can also be change
- **Shadow**: this will apply a faint shadow to the lower right of the text.

7. Select Preview to have a view of the selected font changes on your slide.
8. If you want the highlighted font formatting to be the default for the subsequent text, click the default for the New objects check box.
9. If you wish to accept these modifications, select OK to close and apply the font formatting.
10.

Offset is the percentage the text displays below or above the standard or baseline text. For instance, because the Superscript text is above the baseline, its offset will be a positive number

Making use of Formatting toolbar

You can make use of the Formatting toolbar to use specific formatting characters such as bold, italics, and shadows to highlighted text.

To make use of a particular Formatting, highlight the text you want to format. Click on the toolbar button. Selecting the bold, underline, text-shadow, bullets, and any other character a second time act as the switch removing the formatting. With the drop-down list, you can check out what each font looks like

Replacing Fonts

If you want to change all occurrence of a specific font in your presentation with another font, that can be done seamlessly by doing the following

- Click format, replace fonts. This will make the Replace dialog box opens.
- Choose the font you want to change from the Replace list. You'll only see the fonts present in your presentation listed.
- Choose the font you want to use as a replacement from the drop-down list. In this section, all available fonts are listed.

- Select replace to change all the matching fonts in the presentation
- Click Close to return to the presentation.

Changing Text Case

You can also make the change of text case automatic in your presentation. For instance, your text changes from uppercase to lowercase automatically. To do these follow the steps below:
Highlight the text you want to change, click format, modify the case to the change case dialog box and select the case you want to change your text to. There are several case options which include:

- **Uppercase**: all the letters will be in capital letters.
- **Lowercase**: all letters will be in lowercase.
- **Sentence case**: it will capitalize the first word of every sentence. Just the first word only.
- **Title Case**: In this case, it capitalizes the first letter of all title words. Although some words such as to, for, are exempted from this case and will remain in lower case.
- **Toggle Case**: this case shuffles between all existing cases.

Select ok to put these changes into effect.

Space setting, Alignment, and Indenting

One way you can increase the readability of text on your slides, you may have to adjust the spacing between lines of text and between paragraphs in your presentation. Furthermore, you can also change the indentation and alignment of lines of text. To do these:

- Go to the Paragraph group on the home tab of Ribbon, you'd find several options such as Vertical alignment, Line spacing, and so on

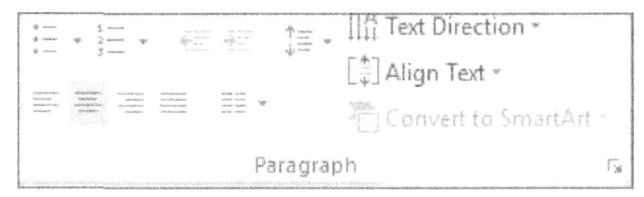

- On the slide, highlight the text you wish to modify.
- Select Home. Go to the paragraph group and select the dialog box launcher.
- The Paragraph dialog box comes up:

Here is a list of options available in the dialog box:

Spacing

- To adjust the spacing below and above a paragraph type or select the arrows beside the before or after. The number can be a decimal or whole number.
- To modify the spacing within and above a paragraph, make use of the line spacing options such as the Single, Double, or 1.5 lines.

POWERPOINT FOR DUMMIES

- Alternatively, you can select and input a specific point value- anywhere between 0 and 1584 in the box.

Note: the bigger the value the wider space.

Furthermore, you can select multiple lines and input a value to the box. Make use of values less than or equal to 9.99. Input a value of 1 is equivalent to single spacing and 3 to triple spacing.

Tip: if you keep inserting lines until you run out of space in a placeholder, the line space font size will be adjusted by AutoFit to contain all list items in the placeholder. As soon as this happens, the AutoFit options will come up. To switch off AutoFit, select AutoFit options, and choose to stop fitting text to This Placeholder.

Indention

To make use of indentions or adjust the number of indentions before a text. Click or input a number in the before text box. Additionally, you can make use of the special options to indent only the first line or to insert a hanging indent. Inches are the measurement unit of Indention and it can be in decimal or whole numbers.

Adjusting Paragraph Text Indent

You can make some adjustments to the spacing of a paragraph first line to create a negative indent or hanging indent or indent the complete paragraph. To do this you can use the view tab or the paragraph section on the home tab depending on which one you want to do and follow these steps

- If the ruler can't be seen at the top of your presentation. Go to the view tab and check the ruler box.
- Select the text you wish to modify and do one of these
- On the horizontal top, the ruler drags the first-line indent marker to indent the first line.
- To have the left indent paragraph increased or decreased. Go to the home tab. In the paragraph section click Decrease list level or increase list level.
- Hanging indent creation- this is where the second lines of a paragraph and the remaining lines that will follow. To do this drag the hanging indent marker to where you want the indention to start.
- **Creating a negative indent**- this is where the text is extended to the left margin. To do this, drag the Left Indent marker to where the paragraph will start.

Changing the Paragraph level of indent

Highlight the text you wish to modify, and do one of these:

- Increasing or decreasing the whole paragraphs left indent.
- On the Home tab go to the Paragraph section select the decrease list level or the increase list level.

Steps to create a hanging indent or first line.

- Click the paragraph or paragraphs you wish to indent.
- Go to the home tab
- Select the paragraph dialog box launcher
- Go to the before box under indention and click the arrow to set the measurement you desire.
- Select the box titled special and select either hanging or the first line
- Click OK.

Alignment

To adjust the horizontal text placement in the alignment box. Select Right, Left, Center, Justified, or Distributed. Justified will insert spaces in between words- this makes the line of text be in contact with both the left and right margins. The only exception is the last line of the paragraph that makes use of normal spacing.

While Distributed is similar to Justified there is a slight difference between because the last line comes in contact with both the right and left margins, with spaces inserted in between words.

NOTE: The distance between the outer border of the enclosing shape or box and the text is the Margin

Specifying Text Direction in a Text box

The direction of the text can be altered in text boxes or shapes. The text in text boxes and shapes can be positioned vertically or horizontally and it can be wrapped to appear in multiple lines or appear in a line. You can alter the text direction and also alter the margins of shapes and text boxes for optimal spacing. You can even make your text appears side that is pivoting your text at 90 or 270 degrees

- Right-click the text box or shape's edge.

POWERPOINT FOR DUMMIES

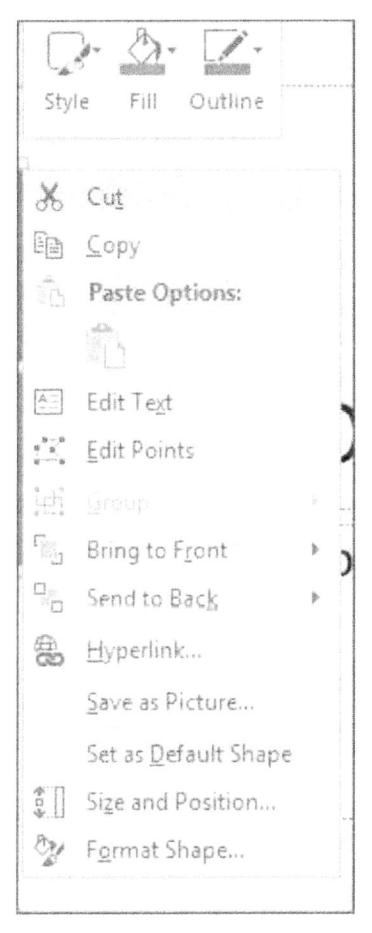

- Go to the shortcut menu, click format shape.
- In the Format Shape section, select size/layouts and properties option
- Beneath the text box, choose the option you want from the text direction list

Format Shape

SHAPE OPTIONS   **TEXT OPTIONS**

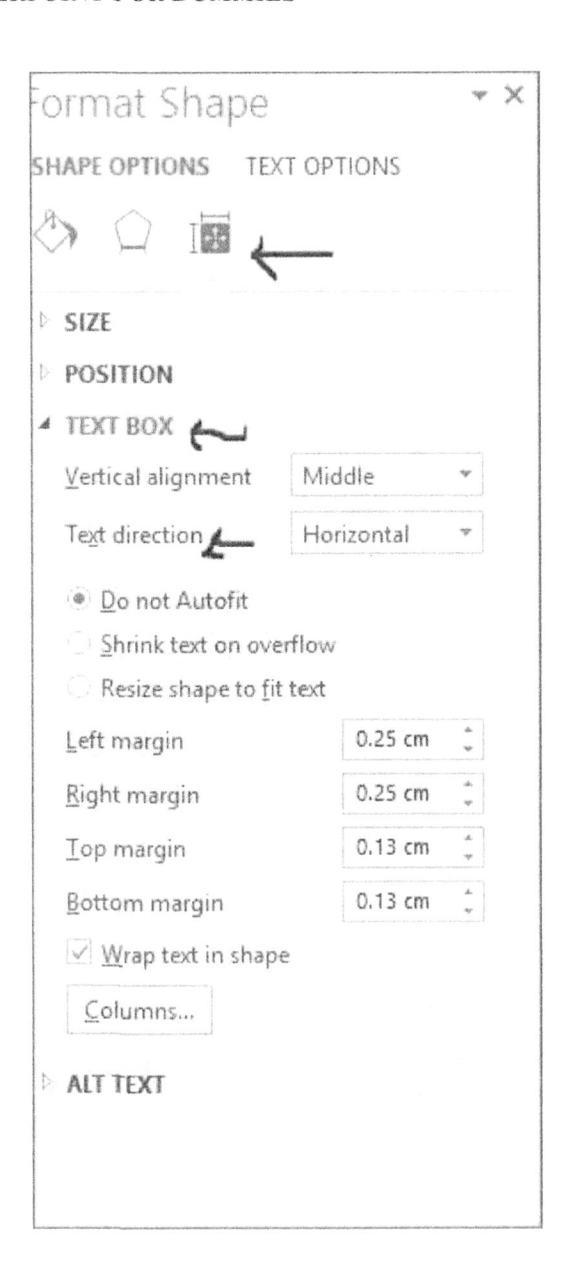

- SIZE
- POSITION
- TEXT BOX
  - Vertical alignment: Middle
  - Text direction: Horizontal
  - ● Do not Autofit
  - ○ Shrink text on overflow
  - ○ Resize shape to fit text
  - Left margin: 0.25 cm
  - Right margin: 0.25 cm
  - Top margin: 0.13 cm
  - Bottom margin: 0.13 cm
  - ☑ Wrap text in shape
  - Columns...
- ALT TEXT

Positioning Text Horizontally in a Text box

To modify the horizontal positioning of a single paragraph or line:

POWERPOINT FOR DUMMIES

- Select the paragraph or line of text that you want to change
- Go to the Home tab
- Pick the horizontal positioning option that you want.

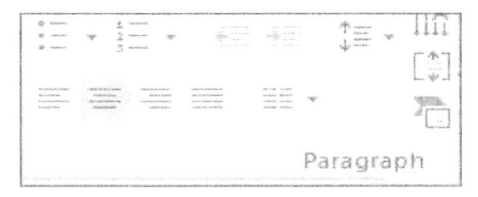

Modifying the horizontal positioning of all text in a shape or text box:

- Select the shape or text box by clicking its border
- Go to the home tab
- Select the horizontal arrangements option you like.

Rotating Text in a Text box or shape

- Add a shape or a text box to your documents
- Type and format your text. Right-click the shape or the text box
- Click Format Shape.
- Click effects under the Format pane
- Enter 180 in the X or Y rotation box found under the 3-D Rotation

The size of Shapes and Text boxes can be automatically increased so that text fits in well.

To do these follow the steps:
- Right-click the text box or shape border
- Move over to the shortcut menu and click the format shape option.
- Under the format shape option, select layout, and properties
- Click Textbox choose the Resize shape option to fill the text.

💡

You can decrease the size of the text to fit into a shape by selecting the Shrink text on overflow

Altering the margin between the edge of a text box or shape and the text.
- Right-click the text box or shape border
- Go to the shortcut menu and select Format Shape.
- Select the size/layout and properties option.
- Pick the option you want in the Vertical alignment list

Right click the text or shape border

Go to the shortcut menu and click on Format Shape

POWERPOINT FOR DUMMIES

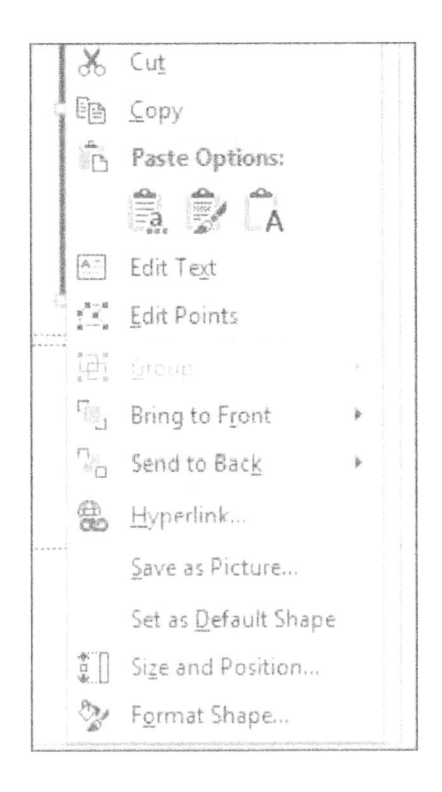

```
Cut
Copy
Paste Options:
Edit Text
Edit Points
Group
Bring to Front
Send to Back
Hyperlink...
Save as Picture...
Set as Default Shape
Size and Position...
Format Shape...
```

In the format shape section select Size/Layout properties

POWERPOINT FOR DUMMIES

Define the measurement in millimetres or inches for any of the margins below:

- Left margin- the distance between the leftmost text and the shape left border
- Right margin- the distance between the right most text and the shapes right border
- Top margin- the distance between the uppermost text and the shapes top border

POWERPOINT FOR DUMMIES

- Bottom margin- the distance between the lowest text and the shapes bottom border

Positioning text vertically in text box

- Right click the shape or textbox's border
- Go to the shortcut menu and select format shape

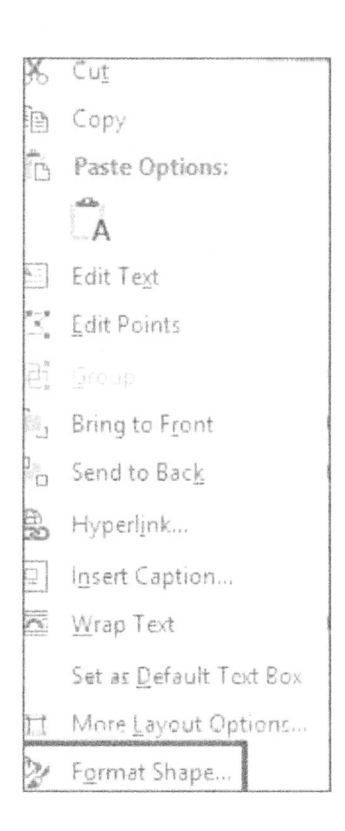

```
Cut
Copy
Paste Options:
    A
Edit Text
Edit Points
Group
Bring to Front
Send to Back
Hyperlink...
Insert Caption...
Wrap Text
Set as Default Text Box
More Layout Options...
Format Shape...
```

- In the format shape section, select Size/Layout Properties

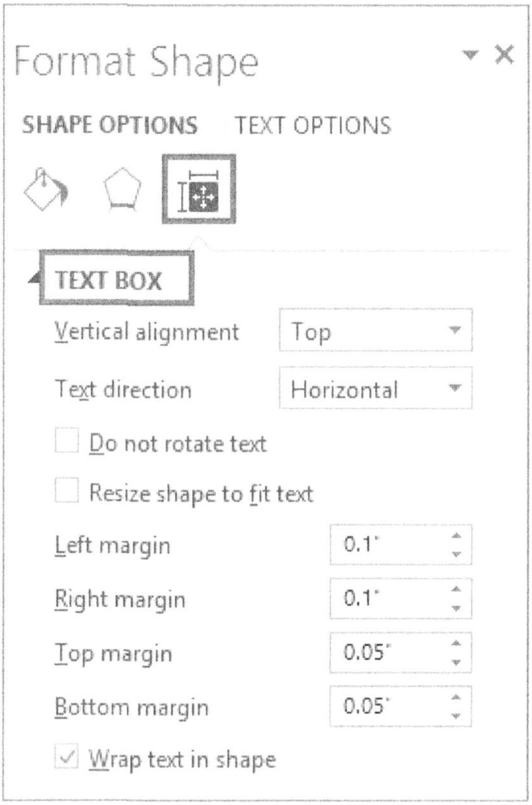
Format Shape
SHAPE OPTIONS
TEXT OPTIONS
TEXT BOX
Vertical alignment
Top
Text direction
Horizontal
Do not rotate text
Resize shape to fit text
Left margin
0.1"
Right margin
0.1"
Top margin
0.05"
Bottom margin
0.05"
Wrap text in shape

- Choose the option you want in the vertical alignment section

Wrapping a text in a text box or a shape

When a text is wrapped, it will by default continue on a new line as it gets to the shape or text box right border.

POWERPOINT FOR DUMMIES

- Right click the border of the text box or shapes containing the text you intend to wrap.
- Go to the shortcut menu
- Click format shape

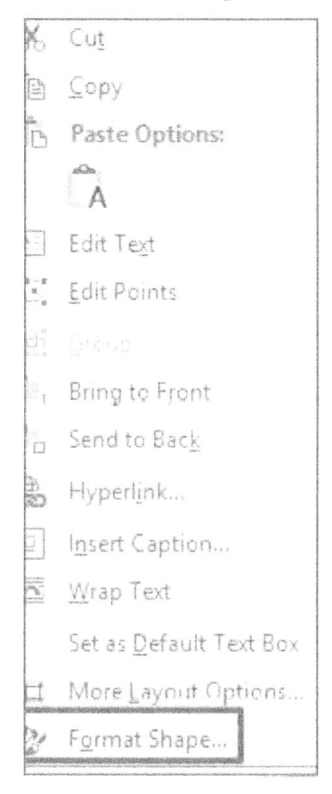

```
Cut
Copy
Paste Options:
    A
Edit Text
Edit Points
Group
Bring to Front
Send to Back
Hyperlink...
Insert Caption...
Wrap Text
Set as Default Text Box
More Layout Options...
Format Shape...
```

- In the format shape section, choose Size/Layout & Properties and click wrap text in shape

POWERPOINT FOR DUMMIES

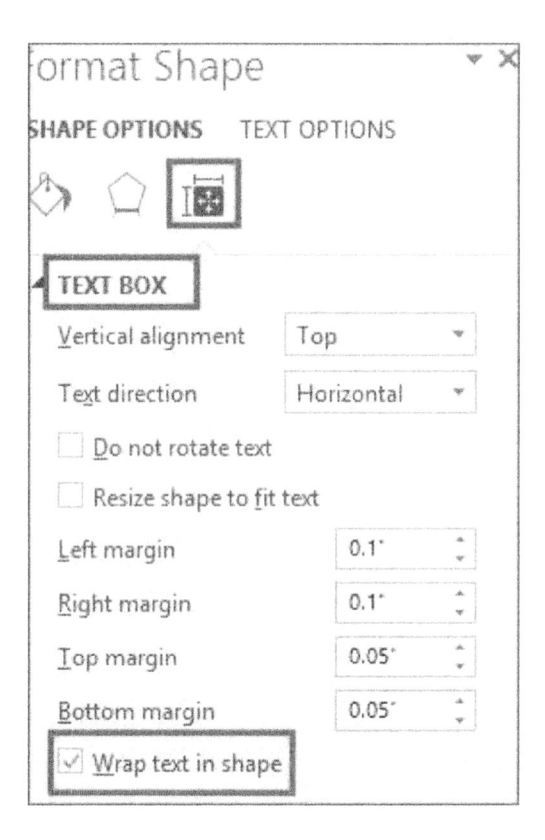

Changing Text Color

To modify the color of texts on a slide, follow these steps:
- Highlight the text you wish to change its color.
- Go to the home tab. Click the font color.
- Select the font color you want to change your text

Changing Text Color of multiple Slides.

POWERPOINT FOR DUMMIES

If the presentation you're creating involves many slides it is better to customize the slide master first. This helps to set the design for other slides ahead of time. So every new slide added will take on the format you want.

Changing the slide master text color will cause changes to text on multiple slides at once.

- Go to the View tab, select Slide Master.
- Move to the thumbnail pane
- On the left choose a layout containing the text you want to modify the color
- Highlight the text on the layout you want to modify
- A toolbar will pop up, click font, and choose the color of the text you want to change to.
- Close Master view to return to your presentation.

If you are not satisfied with the colors available, click more colors, and choose a color on the standard tab. Alternatively, if you are good with colors you can mix colors on the custom tab

Adding bullets or numbers to text

Making use of a numbered or bulleted list will help make your text organization of your text and help to show a sequential process in your presentation. To add bullet to your text

- Go to the view tab, select the normal view under the presentation views group
- Select a thumbnail of the slide you want to add the bulleted or number text to- this you will find on the left side of the PowerPoint window
- On the slide, choose the lines of text you want to add bullets or numbering to- either it's in a table or a text holder
- Go to the Paragraph section on the home tab and click the number or bullet option.

If you want to change all the lines of a text. Click the outline of the text and apply the numbering or bullet

Changing bullet list color

If you are not satisfied with the default color, style, and size of the bulleted or numbered list you can modify it and also choose the point you wish to start from.

For single bullet or number

- Go to the line you want to change and Position your cursor at the beginning of that line

For multiple bullets or number

POWERPOINT FOR DUMMIES

- Highlight the text in the bullets or numbers you wish to modify
- Select Home
- Tap the arrow next to the bullets or numbering option. Select bullets and numbering.

A fast way to change a bulleted or numbered list style is by selecting the style you want in the list that appears beside the bullets or Numbering

Other operations on Bullet and Number List

You can select the style modifications you want to affect by going to the bulleted or numbered tab. Some of the changes you can make include

- Size: to change the size of a bulleted or numbered list of your text, select size and enter a percentage
- Picture: to make use of a picture as a bullet. Go to the bulleted tab, select pictures, and look around to find a picture.
- Starting number: go to the numbered section and input the number you want in the Start at the box.
- **Symbol**: if you want to insert a character to a bulleted list from the symbol list. Go to the bulleted tab and select customize. Choose a symbol you want

POWERPOINT FOR DUMMIES

- Smart Art graphics: to change an existing number or bullet list to a smart Art graphics, select home, and then select convert to smart Art.

Making use of custom styles to multiple slides

The perfect way of applying a custom list to all slides on a presentation is to make the changes in the slide master. Whatever modifications made to the slide master will be automatically saved and will be applied to every slide in the presentation. A single or multiple slide layout can also be created or edited with the layout including your customized list styles and you insert these layouts to your presentation.

PowerPoint List Limitations

As much as you can make use of lists in PowerPoint there are limits to what you can use them for. Here is a list of things not supported on PowerPoint.

- You can't define new number formats. You have the only option of choosing from the default sets of styles that you will find on the Numbered section in the Numbering and Bullet box.
- You can't make use of a decimal numbered list. For example 2.0, 2.1, 2.2 and so on.

- You can't make use of a list that is nested. Although you can make use of the Tab key or make use of the Increase list level option to create the same effect. However, PowerPoint does not automatically set a new indented number style or bullet.
- The bold, italic and underlined formatting cannot be applied to the bullets or numbers. Any form of formatting applies to the highlighted line or list.

Common Problems Faced by Newbies and solutions.

How to change the default bullet character to another one

To change the default bullet character follow these steps
- Go to the view tab and select slide master
- Click the first larger slide in the thumbnail section- this is the Master slide
- Click the Home tab.
- Click one or multiple bulleted lines in the samples.
- Tap the down arrow on the Bullet Icon and pick your default style.
- If there are different bullets for different lines then repeat the process
- After you're through with the update of the bullet styles, Close the master view.

After inserting a text box or slide for bullets, it will appear in your new bullet defaults.

Multi-level Bullets

If you want an indented list with the list follow these steps

- Move your cursor to the beginning of the line you want to work on.
- Then go to the Home tab. In the Paragraph section click increase list level

Moving text to less indented level in the list: Position the cursor at the beginning of the line. Go to the Home tab. In the paragraph section. Select the Decrease list level option.

Stopping the creation of numbers and bullets.

To stop creating bullets or numbers and return to the text, click the bullet or numbering icon again to turn it off.

Alternatively, you can use the Enter and then the Backspace key to erase the number or bullet.

Increasing and Decreasing the Space between Bullet Character and text in a line

If you want to decrease or increase the space that is between a number or bullet and the text in a line. To view the Ruler check box

Position your cursor at the beginning of the line of text. Go to the View tab, in the Show group, select the Ruler check box Drag it to change the space between number or bullets and the corresponding text. We have 3 different types of market that appear on the Ruler. They indicate the indention defined for a text box.

1. **First line indent** – this shows the actual position of the bullet character. If the paragraph is not bulleted shows the position of the first line of text.

2. **Left indent** –maintains the relative spacing of the first line and the Hanging indent markers.

3. **Hanging indent** – this shows the position of the lines of text. In this case, if the paragraph is not bulleted it shows the position of the second line and every line that will come after it.

Bullet coming up after every Addition of a line
Double-check and ensure that the numbers or bullets are in the Text box. In the text, there is always a bullet or number every time you press Enter. To get additional lines without bullets press the Ctrl + Enter keys.

The text in a title box is usually in a single line heading or title. You can make use of bullets or numbers however all lines are treated as a single line by the Text box, which leads to a single number or bullet.

Adjust the indent in a bulleted or numbered list on the ruler

To make changes to the indent in bulleted or numbered lists that is shown on every slide in your presentation, display the slide master, and do the following. Go to the View tab, in the presentation views section, select Slide Master.

1. If the ruler is not displayed, go to the show group on the view tab, click ruler
2. Highlight the numbered or bulleted text that you want to modify

If there are multiple bulleted or numbered items in a text, the ruler will show the indent markers for each level.

3. Do one or more of the following:

- To all the bullets or numbers position move the first-line indent marker.
- To change the text position move the top part of the left indent marker that is pointed.
- Drag the rectangular part on the bottom of the left indent markers to move the indents and still retain the relationship between the number or bullet and the left text-indent as it is.

Repeat steps 2 and 3 for every bullet and number level and every text level you want to change.

Chapter 5

Adding Sauce to your Work

Working with Tables

Presenting data can be quite challenging but it shouldn't have to be complicated. There is no doubt that making use of tables, charts and graphs adds more life to your presentation and makes it easier to understand. In this chapter you'll be exposed to all you need to know concerned ng the use of tables, charts and graph in PowerPoint presentation. Before delving into the advantages and how to make use of tables, charts and graphs let's give a brief description of each.

Tables in simplest terms are data organized into rows and columns. You can display different kind of data by making use of tables. The rows/columns are labelled, so it is easily identified by the reader. How easy tables make your presentation to be understood cannot be overemphasized either it's for business or statistical purposes or whatever the reason is tables sure enhance the understanding of your audience

Adding a table to your PowerPoint presentation is as easy as you can think of. Just head over to the Insert tab and click on Tables and drag

POWERPOINT FOR DUMMIES

your mouse down the number of columns and rows you'll need. You can automatically insert a 10 by 8 table making use of this method. Not satisfied with this? You can manually input the number or rows and columns you want by clicking the insert the table option and type in the numbers out want

While the use of tables can make your presentation amazing the use of graph and charts will make your presentation even more appealing. Of a truth tables look good on a slide, charts can transform multi row and multi column table that covers multiple slides into a single chart on a single slide. With charts you can present complex information in a simple and attractive way. Often time's people find it difficult to tell the difference between a chart and a graph. Well that mean almost the same thing and is used interchangeably this days but there is a slight difference. Not all charts are graphs but all graphs are charts. You can have charts in different forms such as line graph, pie charts and simple bar graph used for comparison of one or two variables and the likes of scatterplots and sunburst used for multiple variables.

To modify the layout or format you'll have to click the table you want to work on to have access to the hidden table tools menu. In this menu you'll have the design and layout tab. If you want to modify the design and appearance of your tab le click on the Design tab. Likewise to modify he layout of your table click on Layout Tab.

You'll find the option of adding more rows and columns in the Layout tab.

Let's move to some formatting operations.

Inserting a table

From the Insert tab, click the Table command. Move your cursor over the grid of squares to choose the number of columns you want. The table will appear immediately on the selected slide. Click on any point in the table, to start typing and add your text. Alternatively you can make use of the tab and arrow keys for easy navigation through the table.

Furthermore, you can insert a table by selecting the Placeholders insert table command

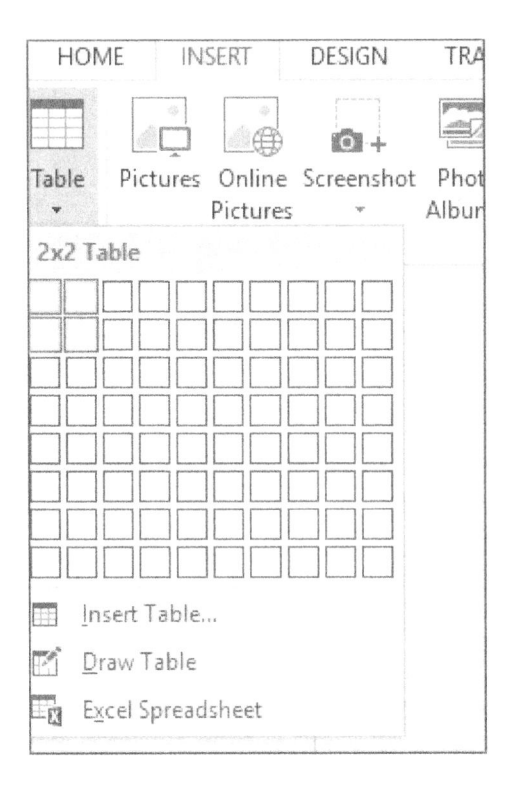

Modifying tables

There are various options for the customization and modification of tables which includes- adding rows and column as well as resizing and moving tables.

Moving tables

POWERPOINT FOR DUMMIES

Select and drag the tables edge to move it to a new point on the slide To resize a table: select and move the sizing handles until you have the desired size

Adding rows and columns

Select a cell adjacent to the point where you intend to add a column or row. Go to the right side of the ribbon and select the layout section. Look for the rows and columns group. To insert a new column choose either Insert right or insert left. If it's a new row choose either insert below or above. The new row or column will appear.

Deleting a row or column

Click on the row or column to be deleted. Go to the layout section and click the rows and columns tab select the delete command and click the delete rows or delete columns option from the menu. The selected row or column will be deleted.

Additionally, you can right click a table to get access to the insert and delete command. Or you select the table's edge you want to work on and press the delete or backspace key.

Modifying tables with the Layout tab

When a table is selected the layout and design tab will come up on the right side of the ribbon. You can make diverse changes to the table by making use of the options on the layout tab.

Customizing the Feel and Look of your Table

It is quite easy to modify the feel and look of your tables. There are different ways of customizing your tables such as modifying the borders of your table, applying different table styles.

- **To apply a table style**: click on any cell I. the table, then select the design tab. Click the table styles group and tap the drop down arrow to see the table styles available. Pick the style you want.
- **To change table style options**: various options on the appearance of the table can be turned on or off. We have six options: Total row, Banded row, Header row, First column, Banded column and Last column. Click any cell in the table. Go to the design tab, and select or deselect the option toy want on the Table style option group.
- **Applying different Table Style options**: there are different table style options and they affect your table style on diverse ways depending on your type of table content

- **Adding borders to a table**: you can insert border to help mark out different table sections. Some table styles may insert borders automatically however adding the borders manually is quite easy. You can modify the border color, border weight etc. Click the cells you want to insert borders. Go to the design tab and choose the line weight, line style and the color of the pen.
- **Customizing the border style**: click the drop down arrow of the border and choose he border type you want.
- Removing borders click on the cells you want to work on abs select the borders command and click no border

One thing to keep in mind while making use of tables is to keep it simple. There's no need in having a table with too many rows and columns, you might end up successfully confusing your audience. If there is a need to present a complex table you can either print it out and give to your audience as handout or more preferably convert it to graph or chat format.

Working with Charts and Graphs in PowerPoint

Inserting a Chart
- On the ribbon, click the Insert tab, and select the Chart command.

POWERPOINT FOR DUMMIES

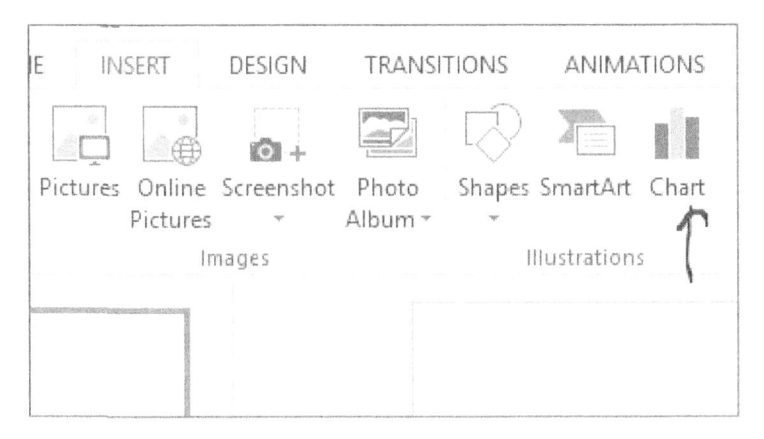

- You'd see a window pop up. Go to the left section and choose a category. Check out the charts on the right pane.
- Choose the chart you want and click OK.
- A spreadsheet and a chart will come up. The placeholder source data is the data appearing in the spreadsheet. It is the data you will use instead of your information.

NOTE: Source data is for chart creation.

- Input data into the worksheet.
- You'd see some data confined by blue lines, these are the only data that the chart will display however this enclosed points will continue to expand as you type.
- When you are through close the spreadsheet and have your chart completed by clicking X.

TIP

You can click on a placeholder insert chart option to add a chart.

Using existing Excel data to create Charts: Have you got an Excel file with some data you intend using for your chart? You can import it making use of the copy and paste feature. Go to the spreadsheet and copy the data you want. Then paste it into the source data area of your chart.

Furthermore you can have an excel chart embedded into your presentation. This can come in handy when you want to have the excel file data updated and at the same time have the chart updated automatically.

Using Chart tools to customize your Chart

There are several ways to organize and customize charts. For instance you can rearrange a chart data, change the style and layout of a chart and even change the chart type.

- **Change the type of chart**: Either you discover that your data won't work well for a type of chart or you feel like making use of another type of chart would be better. Switching to a new type of chart is easy.
- Click the chart you intend to replace.
- On the design tab select the change chart type command. A window would open select the chart type you want and select OK.

At times there might be a need to modify the way your data is grouped. You can switch the rows and columns so as to change the organization of the data

To switch row and column data:

- Click on the chart you want to change, the design tab will come up.
- On the design section go to the data group and click on the edit data command.
- Select the chart again and click on the switch/row option in the data group. You'll have the columns and rows switched.

TIP

In most cases when numbers are inputted in the spreadsheet first column, columns and rows switching can lead to unexpected results. A way to take care of this is to insert an apostrophe in front of every number make the spreadsheet not to format it as a number but as a text instead. For instance 100 should be written as '100

Changing the layout of a chart:

The predesigned chart layout gives you the opportunity to adjust chart elements such as legends, chart titles and the labels of your data to enhance the readability of your chart.

- Click the chart you want to work on.
- Go to the design section and select the quick layout option.
- Choose the predefined layout you want from the options available.
- The new layout will be on chart.
- To modify an element of chart for example chart titles, legends etc. select the element and start typing.

Changing Chart Style

You can easily change the feel and look of your chart style. To change the chart style:

- Click the chart.
- Go to the design section, select the chart style group and click the more icon.
- Click the style you want from the option that appears
- The chart will appear in the selected style.

There are formatting shortcuts buttons for charts. You can use them for the addition of chart element, filtering of data on a chart and changing the style of a chart.

Chapter 6

Adding Sauce to your Work II

Working with Shapes

Inserting a shape:

- Go the insert section.
- Go to shapes in the illustration group. Youd see a window of shapes appear.

POWERPOINT FOR DUMMIES

- Choose the shape you want.
- Select and drag to the desired point to add shape to a slide

Customizing a shape or text box

When you select a shape or a text box handles will appear that will let you tweak the shape. We have various types of handles

- Rotation handle: select and drag the rotation handle to rotate the shapes.
- Sizing handles: Select the sizing handles and drag it till the text box or shape gets to the size you want. To adjust the width and length at the once you can use the corner sizing handle.

  There are shapes with yellow handles- this is used for the customization of the shape. Apart from shapes customizing, rotating and resizing you can also group , order, and align them

Formatting shapes and text boxes.

PowerPoint allow users to customize the shapes and text boxes in diverse ways that can be tailored to suit your project. You can format the shape color, style, and add effects to them and change the shapes into a different shape.

POWERPOINT FOR DUMMIES

Changing the style of a shape

Selecting the style of a shape gives you the chance to apply presets effects and colors to easily mofy the shape and textbox appearance . These options are dependent on the colors that make up your current theme.

- Select the shape or textbox you want to customize.
- Go to the Format section, click the styles group and select the more icon.
- Youd see a menu come up. Choose the desired style. The style will display the shape

Changing the fill color of a shape

- Click the shape or text box to be customized.
- Go to the Format section, select the Shape Fill arrow. The shape fill options will come up
- Hover your cursor the various color available and pick the color you like. Not satisfied? Click the more fill color options to view more color available

- The shape or text box will display in the color you have chosen.

TIP

Click the gradient or texture in the drop down menu to use another kind of fill. Additionally you can make your fill transparent by clicking the no fill option.

Changing the outline of a shape

- Click the shape or text box.

- Go to the Format pane, select the Shape Outline option. A menu will come up immediately.

- Choose the desired . Select the no outline option for a transparent outline.

- The shape or text box will be displayed in the chosen outline color.

TIP

The weight(thickness), and color of the outline can be adjusted in the drop-down menu.

Adding effects of shapes

- Click the shape or text box to be worked on.
- Go to the Format pane, select the Shape Effects option.
- A menu will come up, move your cursor over the effect's style you wish to use, then click the preset effect you want.
- The selected effect will display the shape

TIP

For further adjustments effects of your shape, go to the end of each dialog box and click options. The format shape section will come up letting you tweak the effects.

Changing to another shape

- Click the shape or text box to be changed.
- Go to the Format section, select the Edit Shape option.
- A menu will appear, mover your cursor over the change shape option and choose the shape you want.

Working with SmartArt Graphic

SmartArt gives you the opportunity to coney information with graphics in place of text. There are various kinds of styles to select from, that you can use to explain different kind of ideas.

Inserting a SmartArt graphic

- Click the slide you want the SmartArt graphic to be displayed.
- On the insert tab, go to the illustrations group and select the smartart command.
- A dialog box will come up. Move your mouse to the left and select a category. Select the SmartArt graphic you want and click OK.

POWERPOINT FOR DUMMIES

- After this, the smartart graphic will show on the current slide.

Furthermore, you can insert a SmartArt graphic into a placeholder by clicking the SmartArt command in a placeholder.

Adding text to a SmartArt graphic

Click the SmartArt graphic and a text pane will come up on the left. Enter text beside every bullet in the text pane. The text will be displayed in the corresponding shape. PowerPoint will resize the text automatically to fit inside the shape. Also, you can insert text by selecting the desired shape and start typing.

NOTE: this method will only work if you are adding text to a few shapes. If you are using complex SmartArt graphics it would be better and faster to work in a text pane.

Adding, Deleting and Rearranging shapes:

Adding, deleting and re ordering shapes from your SmartArt graphics is quite easy. All this can be done in the text pane. Let's look at some re arrangement operations:

- **Promoting a shape**: click the bullet you want to work on. Press the backspace key. The shape will move up one level and the bullet will move to the left.
- **Demoting a shape**: click the bullet you want to work on and press the tab key. The shape will move down one level and the bullet will move to the right.
- **Adding a new shape**: place the point of insertion after the bullet you want to work on and press the Enter key. After this a new bullet will come up in the text pane and a new shape will be displayed in the graphic.
- **Removing a shape**: to remove a shape press the backspace key until you have the bullet deleted and the shape will be removed.

Alternatively, if you would not want to organize your SmartArt using the text pane. Go to the "create graphic group" and use the commands on the design tab. Click the shape you want to work on and select the desired command. How to make use of the design tab command.

- **Add a shape**: use this option to insert a new shape to your graphic. Additionally you can click on the drop down option for more positioning options.
- **Move up and move down**: use this option to rearrange the order of shapes that are in the same level.
- Promote and demote: use this option for upward and downward movement of shapes between levels.

SmartArt Customization

After adding a SmartArt, there might be things you want to change about its structure and appearance. Anytime you click a SmartArt graphic, the Design and Format tabs will come up on the Ribbons right side. At this point, it's quite easy to edit and customize SmartArt graphic layout and style.

There are several color schemes you can apply on SmartArt. To customize the color, select the change color option and click the desired option from the menu that comes up. Also PowerPoint has various SmartArt styles that gives you the opportunity to easily customize the feel and look of your SmartArt. To choose a new style click the style you want from the SmartArt styles group.

Furthermore, the shapes can be customized independently. Click any shape in the graphic and select the option you want from the format tab.

Changing the SmartArt layout:

Not satisfied with the way your information is arranged within a SmartArt graphic? Well you can modify the layout to fit your content. To do this: Go to the design tab and click the drop down arrow in the layout group. Select the layout you want. The layout chosen will appear.

NOTE: if the new layout differs too much from the original, a part of your text might not display, so make sure to check the compatibility of the new layout with your content.

Chapter 7

Images, Videos and Animations

Adding images to your presentation is one of the ways to add life to your presentation. Images usually need some modifications such as resizing, cropping to fit into a presentation. Although there are apps with editing features. However they're not easy to learn, the good thing is you do not have to worry yourself as PowerPoint has the image editing most necessary features available. You can insert images into your presentation and even edit them without going through the stress of having a separate picture editing app.

Now let's move on to how you can make use of pictures in your presentation.

How to Insert Images in PowerPoint

Moving swiftly to the addition of images to PowerPoint. Images can be added to your presentation in different ways

Add an image from your computer to your slide

- Click on the point of insertion of the image on the slide.
- Go to the Insert tab, in the images section, select Pictures

- A dialog box would come up, browse for the picture you want to use. Click that picture and select insert.

To select multiple images at once, hold down the Ctrl key while selecting the pictures you want.

Add an image from the web to your slide

- Tap the point insertion of the picture on the slide.
- Select the point of insertion of the image.
- Go to the Insert tab, in the images section select online pictures

Make sure you have Bing showing in the list of sources to search. In the search box, input your search word and press Enter. You can make use of the Size, Color, Layout, and licensing filters to modify the results based on your preferences. Choose the picture you want and select Insert

Paste Images

Pasting an image into PowerPoint is very easy. Just copy the image to your clipboard and right-click at the point of insertion and select the paste option. Alternatively, you can make use of Ctrl + V keys at the point of insertion to insert the image.

Further operations on adding Images

If you want an image to appear on all slides of a particular type, then go to the slide master and add the Image there.

Insert a background picture on a slide
- Right-click the slide's margin
- Click Format Background.

In the Format Background Section select Picture or texture fill. Under the Insert picture, you would get a list of option for the source of your image

- File: add an image from your network drive or your computer
- Clipboard: this adds a previously copied picture. This option will not be available if there is no copied picture
- Online: browse the internet for a picture

To modify the relative lightness of a picture, slide the Transparency bar to the right.

To apply the background image to every slide in your presentation, click apply to all. Alternatively, just close the Format Background Section.

Remove a background picture

Make sure you are in the normal view, click the slide that has the background picture you want to remove

- Go to the Design tab.
- In the customize section click format Background
- In the Format Background section, under Fill, choose Solid Fill.
- Click the down arrow beside the Color button.
- A color gallery will appear. Choose the white color.

The present background will be removed and will be replaced with a white background.

If you wish to apply the changes to other slides in the presentation, select apply to all at the base of the Format Background section

How to Rotate an Image in PowerPoint

If you have an image facing a direction you don't want, PowerPoint has the rotating feature to the rescue.

You can rotate an image 90 degrees at a time by making use of the rotate option on the Picture Tools menu.

To rotate an image, do the following:
- Select the image you want to rotate.

POWERPOINT FOR DUMMIES

- On the Picture tools, click the Format menu. You'd find the rotate button on the right side of Ribbon options. Select rotate Left 90 degree or Right 90 degree.

Alternatively, you select the image that you want to rotate.
- Click the rotation handle- this is at the top of the object.
- Move the image in the direction you want.

Furthermore, you can flip an image. Just imagine it as mirroring an image. If there is a backward image text, you can flip the image to correct it.

To flip your image select the Drawing tool click to k rotate and then flip horizontal or vertical

For more movement options, click the drawing tool select rotate, and click the more rotate options.

After clicking on an image, white circles will pop up on the corners of the picture. Drag and pull one of the circle till you get the size you want. PowerPoint automatically locks the aspect ratio when you resize an image. It means stretching will be prevented when you resize it. If you want to unlock it right-click the image. Select size and position. A menu will come up on the right side. Unselected the lock aspect ratio box

Videos

PowerPoint allows users to add a video and play during presentation. This will add more color to your presentation and make it more engaging. There are also editing features within PowerPoint allowing you to customize the appearance of your video. For instance, you can add effects such as fade in, fade out and also trim the length of your video.

Inserting a video from a file:

There are several ways of adding video to your presentation.

From your PC:

- Go to the insert section and select the drop-down arrow.

- Click the video on my PC option.

- Browse and click the video file you want and select insert

POWERPOINT FOR DUMMIES

Screen Recording Feature: there is a screen recording feature that can help you make a video of whatever is happening on the computer and add it to a slide.

How to make use of Screen recording:

- Click insert and select screen recording
- Choose the area you wish to record. Click on record and start recording your presentation.
- Go to slide show and click on record show and choose if you would like to record from the current slide or from the start.

Inserting online videos:

There are websites that allow users to embed videos into your slides. A video that is embedded will still be on its website. This means the video will not be inserted into the file. Using Embedded video is a way to cut down the size of your presentation file however you'll need an internet connection to play the video on your PC.

Working with videos

- **Previewing videos**: click the video you want to work on. Tap the play/ pause icon under the video. At this point the video starts playing and the timeline beside the play/pause icon will move forward.

- **Resizing a video**: select the video. Move the corner sizing handles around till you resize to your satisfaction.

Note: The video will be distorted if you make use of the sizing handles. So it's best to use the corner sizing because its preserve the original aspect ratio

- **Moving Videos**: select and drag the video to a new point on the slide

- **Deleting a video**: click the video and press the delete or backspace key

Editing and formatting videos

There are several editing options available on the Playback tab.

TIP: most editing features won't work with embedded videos but will work perfectly with videos from an inserted file. Here are some editing operations available

Trimming a video:
- Click the video.

POWERPOINT FOR DUMMIES

- On the ribbon select the playback button. Select the trim video option.

- A menu will come up. You'd see a red and a green handle. The green handle is for setting the start time and the red handle is for setting the stop time.

- Tap the play button to preview.

- After you're through with the trimming click OK

-

Adding Fade in and Fade out effect:

- Find the fade in and fade out command on the play out tab.

- Use the arrows to set fade times or type the timeframe.

Adding a bookmark:

- Select the timeline to get the part of the video you want.

- Select the insert bookmark option on the Playback section. The timeline will display the bookmark immediately.

- Click bookmark to move to that point.

Video options

In the video options group on the playback tab there are options that you can use to choose how your video will play.

- **Volume**: controls the video's loudness.

- **Start**: controls either the video will start when you tap the mouse or if it will start automatically.

- **Play Full Screen**: makes the video display on the whole screen.

- **Hide while not playing**: will make the video hidden when it is not being played.

There are other options that makes it loop until stops and many more.

Video appearance formatting

PowerPoint let users format a videos appearance by applying various effects.

Creating a poster frame:

You can insert a poster frame to your video- this is the placeholder image that will be seen by your audience before the video plays.

- Select the timeline to find the part of the video you want.

- Select the Poster frame option on the format tab.

- Click the present frame from the menu that comes up

- The present frame becomes the poster frame.

Alternatively, you can use a picture from your PC. To do just click the image from File.

Applying a style to Video:
- Click the video.
- Go to the format tab and select Video styles section.
- Tap the more icon to display the video styles that are available.
- Choose the style you want.

Animations

Animating an object:
- Click the object to be worked on.
- Go to the Animations section and select the more icon on the animation section.
- A drop-down menu will come up. Choose the effect you want.

. There will be a small number beside the object to show there is an animation on it. A star character will also appear to the next slide in the Slide pane. Extra effects can be seen at the end of the pane.

Effect options

Some effects have features you can customize to your taste. For instance, you can decide the direction an object comes in from when making use of the Fly in effect. To access these options, go the effect options section under the Animation section.

Removing an animation:

Click the number beside the object and press the backspace or delete key.

TIP

It is best to use Animation moderately, too many of it can even cause a distraction to your audience.

Working with animations

To add more than one animation to an object:

After the selection of a new animation in the Animation section. It will take the place of the object's present animation. However, there might be times you want to add multiple animations to an object. For instance, you might want to use the exit and entrance effect. For multiple animations, you'll select the Add animation option- this will let you adding new animations while keeping the present ones.

Selecting an object:

- Go to the animations sections.

- Under the Advanced animation pane, select the insert animation option to check the animations that are available.

- Click the animation effect you want.

If there are several effects on an object, there will be a number for each effect. This numbers show the order in which an effect will be displayed.

To reorder the animations:

- Click the effect number you want to work on.

- Go to the animations tab and select the Move earlier or Move later option to reorder the animation.

-

Copying animations with the Animation Painter:

You might want to apply an effect to multiple objects. This can be done by using the Animation painter to copy the effects from one object to another

- Select the object with the effect you want.

- On the Animation section, select the Animation Painter option.

- Select the destinatin object for the effects.

To preview animations:

Every animation effects used will display when the slide show is played. However, animations on the current slide can previewed without viewing the slide show.

- Navigate to the slide you want to preview.

-

- Go to the Animations section, and select the Preview option. The current slide animation will play.

The Animation Pane

This allows you to manage the effects on the present slide. With the Animation pane, you can change effect and and even the order effects. This can come in handy when you have several effects.

To open the Animation Pane:

- Go to the Animations tab and select the Animation Pane option.

- A menu will come up on the screen's right side showing present slide effects and the order it will display them.

If there are multiple animated objects, renaming them before you reorder them might be helpful. To rename click the object go to the format tab and click the selection option. Click the object's name twice to it.

Reordering effects from the Animation Pane:

- Go to the Animation Pane, select and drag an effect up or down

- The effects will reorder themselves.

To preview effects from the Animation Pane:

- Go to the Animation Pane, and tap the Play button.

- The current slide effect will play. There will be a timeline on the right side of the Animation pane showing the progress through each effect.

In a case where the timeline can't be seen, click drop down arrow for an effect. Then click the show advanced timeline option.

Changing an effect's start option:

An effect starts playing automatically, when mouse is clicked during a slide show and for multiple effects, you'll have to click multiple times.

However, you can make them play automatically at the same time or one after the other by modifying the start option of each effect. To do this, go to the animation pane and pick an effect. Click the drop down arrow next to the effect and choose one of the three start options.

1) **Start on click:** The effect will start when the mouse is clicked.

2) **Start with Previous:** the effect will start the same time the precious effects start.

3) Start after Previous: as the name indicates when start after the previous effect.

All the effects will be played when you review the animation. You'll have to play the slide show to test effects that are ready to start on click.

The Effect Options dialog box

The effect options dialog box contains advanced options that can be used to fine tune animations. To open the Effect Options dialog box:

- Go to the Animation Pane and click an effect.

- Click the drop-down arrow will come up beside the effect and select Effect Options.

- Tap the drop-down menus and choose the enhancement you want. With this you can insert an effect after the animation is over, insert sound to your animation and even have your text animated in a different order.

There are extra options you can modify in some effects. This varies based on the effect selected. For instance, you change the effects timing. All you have to do is click the timing tab in the effect options dialog box. With this you can insert a delay before the start of the effects, control the number of times the effects applies and even modify the duration of the effect.

Chapter 8

Finalizing your work

After creating your slide youd still have to proofread it and make sure everything is in order. This chapter will be showing you all you need to do after creating your slide.

Using the Spell check Feature

- Go to the Review tab and select the spelling command
- The Spelling menu will pop up on the right.
- PowerPoint will offer suggestions for every error in your presentation. You can choose a suggestion and select change to correct the error

PowerPoint will move from one error to the next till you have reviewed all. After reviewing all errors a dialog box will come up to show the spell check is complete. After that, click OK

If there are it gives no suggestions, you can type the correct spelling manually on the slide

Ignoring spelling "errors"

Sometimes the spell check suggestions are not correct. Words like Proper nouns, Addresses and people's names which may not be found in the dictionary can be marked as Spelling error. However, if any word is marked as an error you can choose not to change it. This can be done in 3 ways

1) **Add**: this will include the word in your dictionary. So it won't be termed as a spelling error again.

NOTE: check the spelling carefully before making use of this option.

2) Ignore: it will skip the word without any change
3) Ignore All: it will skip the word without changes made. Also, every other instance of the word will be skipped.

Automatic spell check

PowerPoint like Microsoft Word automatically checks your presentation for any misspellings, so it might not need a separate check by the spelling command. A red wavy lines in your presentation will show the misspellings. To use the automatic spell check feature:

- Right-click the indicated word. A menu will come up.
- Select the correct spelling from the list of suggestions. It will display the correction in the presentation.
- You can also ignore or add an underlined word to the dictionary.

Modifying proofing options

You can customize your proofing options putting you in firm control of how your text is reviewed. For instance, you can modify the auto spell check feature

PowerPoint allows you to modify the proofing options, giving you more control over how it reviews your text. For example, you can customize the automatic spell check to activate the grammar check- this will help you find contextual spelling errors such "their and they're"

To modify proofing options:

Go to the backstage view. Click options

A dialog box will come up

Click proofing and modify the options as you want. Click OK to save your changes.

POWERPOINT FOR DUMMIES

Modifying proofing or any settings in PowerPoint will affect not just the current presentation but all presentations you edit.

Commenting on presentations

After revising a presentation you might feel some things are missing out and want to add some notes or suggestions without altering the slide.

Leaving a comment let you note something without changing the slide itself.

To add a comment:

- Click the text, object or the point of the slide where you want the comment to be.
- Under the review tab, select the new comment command.
- The comment box will come up, type your comment and press enter or click anywhere outside the box and the comment will be saved.
- A small icon will represent the comment on the slide.

Viewing comments

Returning to the comments pane allows you to view and reply to comments.

- Go to the review tab and select the show comments command or Select a comment icon on the slide

Editing comment:

- In the Comments section, click the comment you want to edit.
- Type the changes you want, and press Enter or click anywhere outside the comment box.
- The changes will come into effect.

To reply to a comment:

- Go to the comments section and select reply under the comments you want to respond to.
- Input your response and press Enter or click on any point outside the box. The new comments will appear under the original comment and there will be an extra icon added to the slide.

Deleting comments

- Click the comment you want to delete.

- Select the Delete command under the Review tab.

For multiple comments. Click the drop-down arrow under the delete command- this allows you to delete comment from your current slide or entire presentation

Comparing presentations

In a situation where you have over one version of a presentation. You can easily compare them making use of the PowerPoint compare feature. Not only can you compare you can also combine them. With this feature you'd see how the presentation differs and know which changes to include in the final presentation

To compare two presentations:

- Open a version of your presentation.
- Click the compare command under the Review tab
- A dialog box will come up. Click the second version of your presentation. Then click merge.
- The revision pane will come up- this allows the comparison of the two presentations

Document Inspector

Anytime you create or edit a presentation, some of your personal info might be added to the slide.

To use Document Inspector:

- Click the File tab to go to the backstage view.
- On the info pane select the check for issues command and click the inspect document option.
- The document inspector will come up
- Click or Unclick the boxes based on what you want to review. Then click inspect.
- On any category a sensitive info is found, there will be an exclamation mark and also a remove all button on each of these categories. Select the remove all option and click close

Protecting your presentation

Unless you protect your document anyone with access to it can open, edit and copy the content. There are various methods of protecting your documents

To protect your document:

- Go to the backstage view by clicking the file tab.
- On the info pane select the protect presentation command.

POWERPOINT FOR DUMMIES

- Under the drop-down menu pick the option that takes care of your needs.

Click the File tab to go to the backstage view. From the Info pane, click the Protect Presentation command. In the drop-down menu, choose the option that best suits your needs. A dialog box will come up. Click OK to save. Another dialog box will pop up and click OK again.

There are different options such as the Mark as final option- once you click this option it will appear at the top of your presentation to discourage other users from editing the documents. However this won't stop anyone from editing it will only discourage them. Anyone who would still like to edit can do that by just clicking the Edit option. To totally stop anyone from editing the content of your document use the Restrict access option.

POWERPOINT FOR DUMMIES

Chapter 9
Now that you are done

After creating your presentation you might be think of the vest format to save it. PowerPoint gives a variety of options to its users.

Printing your presentation

- Click file and select print.

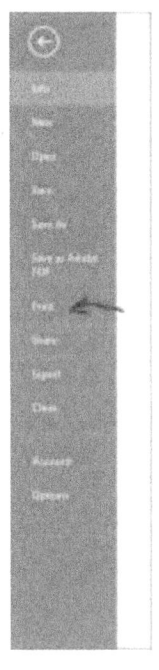

For printer, choose the printer you want to use.

POWERPOINT FOR DUMMIES

- For settings, choose any of these options: Slides, Print layout, Collated, Color, Edit header to modify your presentation.
- Select how many copies you want to print.
- Click Print.

Creating a PDF

PowerPoint allows you to convert your presentation to PDF or XPS so you can share with others. Follow the steps below to create a pdf

Click the Create PDF/XPS button.
- Input a name in the file name box, if the file hasn't gotten a name already.
- Under the save as type list click the *pdf option
- Select the open file after publishing check box if you want the file to open in the chosen format after saving
- Select standard if the document needs to be of high quality. Otherwise if having a smaller size is of more importance select the Minimum size option

Click options to select the pages you want to print, decide if you want the markup printed and choose the output options. Click OK to finish the selection and Click Publish

Saving your presentation on USB flash drive or CD

You can save your presentation on CD or USB drive so that others can watch your presentation. Follow the steps below to do these

1) Insert an empty CD (CD-R), a CD-RW with a replaceable content or an empty rewritable CD (CD-RW) in the disk drive

2) Open PowerPoint. Click file and select Export.

3) Under export select package presentation for CD option.

4) Click package for CD

5) The package for CD menu will come up, input a name for your CD in the box

6) Adding presentations: Click add choose the presentation and click add again. Do this for every presentation that you intend to insert.

POWERPOINT FOR DUMMIES

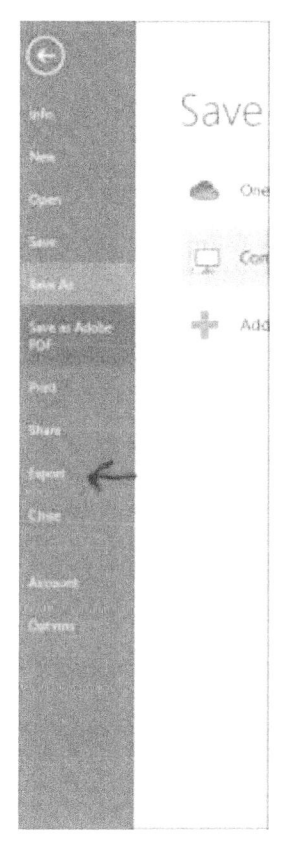

Tip: if you add multiple presentations. The order in which PowerPoint arranges them in the "Files to be copied" list will determine the order in which they play. To reorder the list make use of the arrow button on the dialog box's left side

If you want to add additional files for instance, Linked files or true type fonts, click options.

In the Include these files section tick the boxes you want and select OK to close the menu.

Save your package to a USB flash drive

Click the file tab, select export and tap the Package Presentation for CD and select Package for CD. Under the Package for CD section, select copy to Folder. Under the copy for folder select browse. Repeat process 2-7 and do the following

- Under the location section browse the options and select your USB flash drive
- Click on it or a sub folder in it. Click select.
- The path and the folder you select will be added to the Folder dialog section under location box subsection.

There are a series of questions PowerPoint will ask regarding linked files. Answer yes to all the questions- this ensures that every necessary file are added to the package saved to the USB flash drive

Tip: Although you can choose not to answer yes to all the questions based on preference it is better to click yes to all questions.

After this PowerPoint copies the files and when completed a window displaying the complete package on the USB flash drive would come up.

Save as Video

After creating your slides, adding all the features you're ready to create a video file. To do these:

- Save your work on the File menu to ensure you have your recent work saved in PowerPoint presentation formation. (.pptx)
- Click the file tab to go to the backstage view. Select Export and click create a video.
- Alternatively go to the Ribbons recording tab, select Export to video. Under create a video heading click the first drop-down box and the quality of the video you want (the resolution). The higher the quality the larger the size of the file. Here is a table showing the options available

Option	Resolution	For Dispaying on
Ultra HD(4K) on windows 10 only	3840 by 2160	Large monitors
Full HD	1920 by 1080	Computer screens
HD	1280 by 720	DVD and Internet
Standard	852 by 480	Portable devices

POWERPOINT FOR DUMMIES

The second drop-down box in create a video heading shows if your presentation has your timings and narrations included. The default value will be "don't use recorded timings and narrations" if you have not recorded a timed narration.

Except you change the time spent on each slide, the default time is 5 seconds. To change the timing spent on each slide box. Make use of the arrows on the right side of the box to decrease and increase the duration. If there is a timed narration previously recorded, the value "use recorded timings and narration" and do these:

- Click Create Video
- Input a filename in the file name box and select the folder that will contain the file
- Click save
- Choose either the MPEG 4 video or Windows video format

You can monitor the creation of a video process by looking at the bottom of your screen to check the status bar. Creating a video might take up to hours depending on the complexity and duration of the presentation

To play your created video, go to the folder location, and double-click the file.

Save as a PowerPoint Show

If someone opens a PowerPoint Show file, it will display on full-screen in Slide Show, and won't be in edit mode. The viewer will start watching the video immediately.

To ensure your recent work is saved as PowerPoint presentation format

- Go to the file menu and click save
- Go to the file menu and click Save As.
- Select the folder location where you want your file save
- Choose PowerPoint show (*.ppsx) in the Save as options.
- Click save.

Chapter 10
Work like a Guru

Now that you know how to make use of PowerPoint this chapter will be exposing you to tips that will make your PowerPoint experience easy and seamless.

7 Quick tips to make your Presentation more effective

1) **Keep it simple**: do not try to make it things too complicated while trying to be creative.
2) **Always save your work**: as you create your presentation always ensure to save your work, you dont want to be in a situation where you have done a lot of customization and you discover you didnt save it
3) **Highlight what important**: this is a way of effectively passing out your message to your audience.
4) **Use high quality pictures**: PowerPoint is all about presenting an information visually. Using quality will aid pictures this process.

5) **Use the right font**: using PowerPoint is not to showcase fanciful fonts except if needed. Make use of font that are easy to read.
6) **Use the right color**: except if it is very important. There is no need to mix colors and even if you would make sure you are mixing the right color.
7) Make sure all objects are properly aligned.

PowerPoint shortcut

Here are some shortcuts that mright come in handy when working on PowerPoint

For windows

Shortcut	Use
Ctrl + N	New Presentation
Ctrl + S	Save presentation
Ctrl + X	Cut selected text or object
Ctrl + C	Copy highlighted text, object or slide
Ctrl + V	Pate
Ctrl + Z	Undo last action
Alt + N,S, H	Insert a shape

Alt + N, P	Insert a picture
Alt + H, L	Select a slide layout
Page down	Go to next slide
Alt + N	Go to insert tab
F5	Start slide show
Esc	End slide show
Alt + G,H	Select a theme
Alt + H,F,S	Change font size
Ctrl + M	Add new slide
Ctrl + B	Make text bold
Alt + W,Q	Open the zoom dialog
Ctrl + Q	Close PowerPoint

For MacOS

Shortcuts	Uses
Command key + N	New Presentation
Command key +S	Save Presentation
Command key +X	Cut highlighted text or object
Command key +V	Paste text or object
Command key +Z	Undo
Command key + B	Make text bold

POWERPOINT FOR DUMMIES

Command key + C	Copy highlighted text or object
Command key + Q	Close PowerPoint

POWERPOINT FOR DUMMIES